SEWARD HILTNER

The Counselor in Counseling;

CASE NOTES IN PASTORAL COUNSELING

ABINGDON PRESS
Nashville • *New York*

The Counselor in Counseling

ISBN 0-687-09754-1

Library of Congress Catalog Card Number: 52-375

PRINTED AND BOUND AT NASHVILLE,
TENNESSEE, UNITED STATES OF AMERICA

To

My Father and Mother

CLEMENT SEWARD HILTNER
CHARLOTTE PORTER HILTNER

FOREWORD

Counseling takes place in a relationship between parishioner and pastor. Relationship, parishioner, pastor —all must be studied. And the greatest of these, from the point of view of what we can do to improve our counseling, is the pastor, for the simple reason that we have access to ourselves. If we change ourselves, we automatically change the potentialities in the relationship and, therefore, the possibilities of help for the parishioner.

Especially in the teaching of counseling to ministers and theological students I have come to feel that learning about our own attitudes in counseling is the most subtle but most important aspect of our task. Learning about the parishioner, his immense varieties and unique individualities, is of great importance. But we may know all about the parishioner and still be unable to enter into a fruitful counseling relationship. To paraphrase Paul, we may have all knowledge — of something out there, an object detached from us — and yet we may well be nothing — if we are without a genuineness that comes only from penetration into our own attitudes.

Suppose that a counselor learns something about himself and his own attitudes as these have been expressed in his counseling. For instance, let him realize, on analyzing a pastoral contact, that he gave a belligerent or an anxious

7

impression to the parishioner even when this was not his conscious intention. He then sees what he had not seen before, that belligerency or anxiety was in his attitude despite his ignorance of this fact. He will be chagrined but illuminated. His later counseling will be better because his insight has led him to a negative factor in his attitude which, once clearly viewed and dealt with, is no longer an obstacle.

Or let the counselor on some occasion, when truly puzzled, confess this fact honestly to the parishioner. He may then discover, to his amazement, that the parishioner at once makes a stride ahead. On reflection the pastor sees that something inside himself had a faith and trust in the parishioner which was even deeper than he knew in his head. He realizes that this confidence communicated itself to the parishioner even before he himself could identify it. The insight in this situation has been positive, revealing previously unsuspected resources in one's own basic attitude toward and feeling for the persons he tries to help.

Whether the insight into ourselves is positive or negative, it is equally valuable for the improvement of our counseling if we accept, understand, and assimilate it.

It is not true that the best approach to improving our counseling is merely learning more and more about the people we try to help. This is indispensable but only partial. Fully as important is the discovery of hidden strengths and obstacles in ourselves. We may still "see through a glass, darkly," since people, including ourselves, are complex creatures. But we can at least make efforts to scrape some of the black paint off the glass.

It should be noted, however, that these personal insights emerging from our counseling experience are not the same as analyzing ourselves as total personalities. My discussion limits itself to those attitudes of the counselor which appear in the bit of counseling experience being studied. Thus the insights are limited. My focus is on those insights which affect us as professional workers and which emerge from our professional experience — not on the deeper and more total insights into us as complete persons or selves. If there proves to be some therapy in such self-examination for professional purposes, it is a mere by-product and also incomplete.

If I had sat down to write a completely systematic and comprehensive book about the counselor's attitudes in counseling, I should probably never have got beyond page one. Few people, and certainly not I, are equipped at this stage of our knowledge to write a systematic book on this subject. But when I relieved myself of the need to be all-inclusive, I found the book could be written. For it is based entirely on the implications of actual counseling experiences.

I believe that this case analysis approach may prove more helpful to readers than would a systematic but more abstract discussion. Because of the concrete material one chapter may succeed in touching a reader at the point of his own concern. A different chapter may prove meaningful to a second reader. In either case, the reader may then be better able to find his own ways of increasing the understanding of himself which he needs for better counseling.

For a comprehensive statement of my approach to pastoral counseling the reader is referred to my previous volume, *Pastoral Counseling*. Below I present a few points which are fundamental in my general approach.

1. A true counseling situation exists when a parishioner recognizes that something is wrong, senses that this is in some measure within him, and is convinced that a professional person may be able to help him with it, not by giving him the answer but by aiding him to clarify it for himself. The criterion of counseling lies, therefore, not in the intention and attitude of the pastor but within the readiness and need of the parishioner.

2. Most of the pastor's professional contacts are not counseling in the narrower sense but are precounseling pastoral work. The attitude of the pastor is the same in both instances. But the need or readiness of the parishioner is different. One is no more important than the other within a total ministry.

3. The best word to characterize the attitude and approach of the pastor in counseling and precounseling pastoral work is "eductive." The pastor does not coerce, moralize, push, divert, or direct. Instead he attempts to lead out or draw out resources and strengths which can become operative only as they are helped to well up within the parishioner. The eductive approach implies an acceptance and understanding of what the parishioner is pre-

pared to communicate, not in the sense of agreement but in receiving this as the material which must be examined if clarification is to be achieved. This approach is not passive. It does involve much mirroring of feelings expressed. But it also includes frequent definition and redefinition of the counseling situation. The counselor is a person, not a mere bit of machinery.

4. Counseling is not a mechanical process, but an interpersonal relationship in which two people concentrate on clarifying the feelings and problems of one and agree that this is what they are trying to do.

5. In terms of basic attitude, approach, and method, pastoral counseling does not differ from effective counseling by other types of counselors. It differs in terms of the setting in which counseling is done, the religious resources which are drawn upon, and the dimension at which the pastor must view all human growth and human problems.

6. The improvement of pastoral care and counseling involves both practical and theoretical study and the interrelationship between them. The two essential bodies of theoretical knowledge are theology, broadly conceived, and dynamic psychology, similarly viewed. The practical knowledge is observation of all the kinds of actual situations in which the pastor tries to help people.

I am indebted to the ministers and theological students whose experience as counselors-in-training has supplied much of the concrete material to be found in these pages. They, as well as their parishioners, have furnished the cases without which such a book could not be written.

I am deeply indebted to *Pastoral Psychology* magazine and to its editor, Simon Doniger, both for encouragement and help in writing this book and for permission to use some material which was originally published in that valuable magazine.

This book is written for my fellow ministers. But since it is my conviction that the basic dynamic principles of counseling are the same for all professional groups, I hope it may also have relevance for some others who do counseling in the course of their professional work.

SEWARD HILTNER

CONTENTS

13

ACTION IN COUNSELING

Chapter One

J

T MUST BE NO LATER THAN CHAPTER 2, VERSE 1, of *I Counseling* where it is written, "Action is no substitute for clarification." The early appearance of this principle in our learning does not, however, make it easy to follow.

Even the scantiest kind of observation suggests to us that most counseling situations which begin with a wrestle over an action decision do not get far if they remain only at that level, if they fail to explore the feelings which lie beneath each possible action.

A teen-ager is torn between going to Northwestern or Northeastern. We suggest that he tell us how he feels about them. When it appears that one is in his home town and another at some distance, and the conflict is about his relationship to his parents and getting emotionally away from home, we may be able to help him clarify. If we can, the chances are that the decision for east or west will be made without much difficulty.

This does not mean that action decisions are automatic once the emotional underbrush has been hacked up. There remain the stubborn questions of value. But once some understanding and clarification have been achieved concerning the inner, and hence partly concealed, issues, decisions on actions become possible, if not easy.

Nor does it mean that anyone who begins to talk with us about an action decision can be induced to talk about what lies behind it instead, or that we should always get him to do so. The underlying feelings may be dynamite from his point of view, and he may be literally unable to talk about them. In any event, we do not urge. Sometimes our dealings with parishioners need to be watchful waiting. We may see that they have a problem they can begin to solve only if they can discuss it in terms of causes and not solely of symptoms, but we may have to wait a long time before hope or desperation gives them the courage to do so. In such cases the waiting is not fraught with impatience on our part if we know what we are doing.

The siren of the action piece seems to be the counseling experience—we have all had one like this—in which we find ourselves forgetting our principles, getting on the action band wagon, and appearing to get positive results. We may then be lured into bad practice and bad theory because of insufficient analysis of what happened when we seemed to get good results.

Such a case is that of Joseph Benton and his pastor, Arnold Stone. Mr. Benton is in his thirties, works in a firm owned by his family, and bears the nickname "Zip" from his drive and enthusiasm. He was in the middle of professional training when drafted into the Army. After

16

several years' service he entered the family business instead of completing his professional education.

He married while in the Army and now has three children. His wife has not been very well since the birth of her third child and worries about raising her children in Bigtown. The Bentons are all active church members.

Mr. Benton once invited Mr. Stone, his pastor, to attend a sporting event; but this had to be canceled because of other duties which arose for them both. When Mr. Stone was invited again, he made a special point of accepting and of protecting the time. Mr. Stone drove Mr. Benton to the stadium. Here is the way Stone describes what then happened: "In a few moments I noticed a change in his disposition. He suddenly left off his conversation. His face grew pale and white. He was guarding the fact that he was breathing with difficulty. As the game started, the noise of his breathing grew worse. I sensed him to be in great suffering. I turned to him inquiringly."

BENTON: I'm afraid I'll have to leave. I feel sick.
STONE: That's too bad! Sure thing, let's get out into the open air immediately.

Benton was shaky, and Stone gave him a hand getting out of the stadium and into the car.

STONE: You should be much better soon. What do you think troubles you?
BENTON: I should have known better than to try to come to-

17

day. I guess I'm not quite up to par. And anyway, I just can't take excitement since the war. I thought I should try to control myself. I failed. I really am sorry to have ruined your afternoon. Won't you go back in and let me go on home? I can make it all right. I'm much better now.

STONE: No indeed! I have a little confession to make too. I was feeling the effects of the tobacco smoke, and the screaming didn't help me either. I am glad we are leaving. How are you feeling now? Better?

BENTON: Yes. (*With new strength in his voice*) I'll be O.K. now. I'd like to talk to you, but I don't guess this is the time for it in all this traffic. But I've got to do something soon or crack up. It is pretty bad. This attack of nerves, I mean.

STONE: Do you really think it is as bad as that?

At first Stone performed the necessary job of getting Benton out of the stadium and on the way home. His repeated suggestions to Benton that he is better are understandable. But this last remark is of a different order. To suggest that he may not be so bad as he thinks is one thing while an acute attack is on. To doubt whether his whole situation is as bad as he believes it is, is something else.

BENTON: I am sure of it. Why, do you know that I have hidden my condition for some years? My wife is the only one who knows what I endure. Take this, for example. I haven't been in to the heart of the city for a year. I'm afraid of the traffic, of crowds, of noise. I even drive down a less traveled street rather than risk the through routes. And it isn't all just nerves. I've probably got a bad heart or something else seriously wrong. I hate to think what it may be.

Whatever else Benton has shown up to this point, it is at least certain that he is the victim of acute anxiety. But this anxiety has just shown itself in a fairly open attack, which makes it all the more unlikely that he is full of somatic ills as he says. We know that the first thought of a person feeling anxiety of this kind is to try to peg it, find a "good reason" for his feelings, and that this is often in the form of suspected somatic conditions. Suppose Benton did have a bad heart. Then when anxiety arose, he could say, "My feeling bad is mainly my heart." This means that he does not feel responsible for his heart but does feel so about the anxiety. Meanwhile, the anxiety would go on; and nothing would be gained.

STONE: What does your doctor say is the matter?

Here is the first obvious turning to action. A good counselor might have said, "The whole thing seems pretty bad to you." Instead, Stone begins on action.

BENTON: (*laughing nervously*) That's another of my fears. I've not seen a doctor since I got out of the service. If I went to see one, he'd probably hospitalize me or make me go away for a long rest. You see, my family needs me here, and we couldn't get by without my income. I've just got to stick it out some way for a while longer. Do you see my point?

19

STONE: Yes, I do. You certainly are right in thinking of your family. But will this really solve your problems? We agree that they need you very much. Perhaps a checkup would reveal that you have nothing seriously wrong, that treatment without a rest or layoff from work will be all that is necessary. A checkup would show just what your trouble is, and you would be wise to see a doctor in the morning, don't you think?

BENTON: But what if he does find that I have an ulcer or a heart condition or something like my wife seems to think I might have? What could I do about it? Don't think I wouldn't like to leave Bigtown. It's no good for me. But I can't leave my job. I am not financially able.

STONE: Perhaps you are anxious about the seriousness of your illness without reason to be. Nervousness is often caused by emotional states or some functional disturbance rather than for causes you have mentioned.

BENTON: Yeah, I know that is right. I have heard that one out of every two prescriptions filled in Bigtown is for nerves. But another factor is that I am losing weight. Doesn't that indicate there is something wrong with me physically?

STONE: Of course it might be caused from something organically wrong, but in your case it is unlikely. You have told me tonight that you are distressed financially, that you have emotional stress in crowds, and dislikes of your town; and since your work involves lots of driving in traffic, you are saying your job is not too desirable in your estimation. These anxieties would cause you to lose weight. Your upset nerves cause poor appetite and bad digestion and numerous other troubles that will reflect in a loss of weight. For instance, you may be suffering from an anemic condition or low blood pressure that is causing you grief. These or other simple troubles can be quickly corrected by medication. A trip to your doctor would likely make a new man of you.

BENTON: Say, that really makes me feel relieved. I guess I have been a little childish about all this. I had just built it up in my mind that I would have to have at least an operation or worse. After what you have said it makes it easier. I'll make an appointment for a checkup in the morning. I'll surprise my wife and not tell her about it until afterward. (*pause*) But I just thought of something else. Do you think I might have to take any shots? I used to faint away when they gave us shots in the Army.

STONE: I know many people who dread a needle. I am glad to tell you that likely you would not be subjected to shots, for most medicine can be given by mouth with fine results if shots bother you. I really am glad you have decided to see a doctor. He will have more time with you than our Army doctors had. Besides he will know you have come to him because you wanted to and will have no reason to doubt your purpose. You remember all the gold-bricks we had in the Army?

BENTON: I surely do. Well, I guess we've been parked here long enough. Come on in.

STONE: Thanks, but I need to be getting home. Glad you are over your upset. Don't forget that promise for tomorrow.

Stone reports that Benton kept his promise and saw a physician. The doctor found him anemic, and with some other minor bit of difficulty. Ten days later he had been taking the doctor's prescriptions of tonic and vitamins and had gained six pounds. Stone writes, "He appears to have a firm grip on his hopes of gaining his health back without having to lose face at the office and at the same time discharge his family obligation as a bread-winner. I saw a marked change in Zip in these few days."

Stone made no attempt to analyze or evaluate the contact other than to indicate that it took place under trying conditions since he was driving the car in heavy traffic during most of it. The absence of analysis can be attributed in part to the fact that he planned to turn it in to me, and no doubt suspected that I would raise questions about the action. But in his mind he had got results, for Benton began to get better as soon as he saw the doctor.

We may look first at what has actually happened to Benton. As a result of this contact he has seen a doctor, discovered he has no dread disease, and has taken some pills. He may well have needed the tonic and vitamins; but in any event, taking them gives him the feeling that he is building up his health. He has no grounds now for fearing that he has an ulcer or heart disease. For the moment he feels much better, and this is reflected in the six pounds of weight increase.

But nothing has been done about his anxiety except a certain diversion of it. The one solid thing we can see is that he did visit the doctor; and even if this was almost on order from Stone, still he did it himself. There has been, so to speak, a temporary arrest of the vicious anxiety circle: feel bad, fear illnesses, acute attack, feel worse, and so on.

If, therefore, Stone's activity had been directed toward getting a break within the circle so that Benton could then begin to look at his anxiety, we might consider his methods a bit rough but understandable. But this is not what Stone has tried to do. Instead, his getting Benton to the doctor has been a substitute for counseling. Now that Benton has made one move in going to the doctor, he might be in better mood for counseling. But Stone does not have this in mind.

Yet Benton's anxiety keeps on churning; and once the novelty of the pills has worn off, he will undoubtedly begin to feel bad again. This time he cannot easily blame it on a possible heart or ulcer. He may feel worse than ever. For when the acute attack had broken down his defenses and he talked with Stone, all Stone did was to urge him to visit a doctor. He has done that, got his health a little better, but he really feels worse than before.

Stone might have reasoned this way: "I can see that what he gets from a doctor may be good and necessary, but still only a palliative in relation to the basic condition. But I don't believe I have either time or experience enough to get far into this. I'd better go easy." This would be understandable. But he did not go easy. He went all out for what a physician could do. Letting Benton say as much as he felt able to about the anxiety itself would have hurt nothing, whether he felt he could go on with it or not.

Thus the evil is not necessarily discussing action if we know we have deserted counseling itself when we do so. It is in resorting to action-discussion as a substitute for clarification; and then, by a superficial evaluation of results, fixing ourselves in a practice which, whatever its bright immediacies, will do harm to our people and our own counseling in the long run.

Another brief illustration may help. Peter Bosse is an active member of a church young people's group. Peter's mother, who believes that the more church services one attends the better he is, is constantly urging Peter to attend more functions. Peter rebels, although he does attend a good many. On the evening of the annual church meeting Mrs. Bosse approached the young minister.

PASTOR: Good evening, Mrs. Bosse. Fine to see you out tonight.

MRS. BOSSE: Good evening. You know, I want to talk to you about Peter. Last Wednesday night James invited him to a party when he knew we were having a midweek Lenten service that evening. Peter went, especially because he knew a certain girl was going to be there. And I don't think that's right!

PASTOR: I know how you feel, Mrs. Bosse. You believe he should have been at the service that night, especially when the young people were sponsoring it.

MRS. BOSSE: Yes, I do. But I didn't dare say much to Peter because I saw you weren't there.

PASTOR: Yes, I'm sorry. I was on vacation for four days and didn't get here.

MRS. BOSSE: (*apparently relieved*) Oh, yes, I knew you would attend unless something came up. But what I'm worried about is that Peter is coming for the supper tonight and not staying for the meeting. James has purposely planned another party tonight, and Peter is going. I don't like it at all.

PASTOR: Of course not. Do you want me to talk to Peter?

MRS. BOSSE: Yes, that would be fine. I think you could make him see it's wrong, but don't tell him I talked with you.

PASTOR: No, Mrs. Bosse, I won't. He's old enough to think these things out.

MRS. BOSSE: Then you'll speak to him for me? That's fine.

PASTOR: You bet. I'll see what we can do.

The pastor wrote of this, "I think the passive method was best here. I tried to play ball with both her and her son without being a hypocrite."

This situation also is so handled that it gets over the immediate unpleasantnesses. The pastor reports that he talked with Peter, without reprimand, and the conversation wandered to Peter's future occupation. But even if immediate unpleasantness has been cleared up, and the pastor's relationship with Peter not ruined, he has connived with Mrs. Bosse at precisely the wrong points. Why could he not have said to Mrs. Bosse, "I take it you've talked with Peter about this and he doesn't agree"? After she has castigated Peter again, why not, "If I understand you correctly, you're worried not only about Peter's not coming to the meeting, but also about him in general and his feeling toward you"? This might be too direct. But his unwillingness to try to define the situation puts him in a hypocritical position and permits Mrs. Bosse to work him. His getting out of the immediate situation by offering to talk with Peter is making action a substitute for clarification.

If we analyze honestly those situations in which resort to action or action-discussion seems to have got results, we find invariably that they have something in common with the Benton or the Bosse relationships, unless the action-discussion has followed a clarification of emotional issues. The moral of the story is, then: if you think action has got results, analyze it more deeply.

EXTERNALS IN COUNSELING

*I*T IS NOT EASY TO KEEP OURSELVES FROM BECOMing preoccupied with externals in pastoral counseling. When we are engaged in precounseling contacts of many kinds, it is even harder.

To focus our attention on externals is the opposite of concentrating on the basic thing—feeling or attitude—which the parishioner is trying to convey to us. It usually occurs because some interest or knowledge of ours is touched by what the parishioner says, and instead of responding to him we respond to the idea which has touched the button in us. This diverts our attention from him as a person trying to communicate something.

Let us suppose that I am a pastor engaged in counseling, that I happen to be a tuba player for recreation, that my son collects stamps, that my wife enjoys walking around our house on her hands, and that I have an aversion to men with red hair whose names are Sam. If, then, my parishioner says, "That's the way it is. We'll be sitting at a play or a movie or a concert, and something will happen—like the bull fiddler breaks a string—and she starts crying right then and there. I just get out, that's all. What's the difference if all the instruments break, even the tuba?" He seems to be expressing resentment and perhaps guilt, so my response should probably be something like, "You mean it's hard to understand and even harder to take?" But if music and tuba have touched me hard, I might say instead, "You're being kind of hard on the orchestra, aren't you?" This would be fine in dinner conversation, but diverting in counseling. Or I may be more subtle, saying merely, "Tell me more about these occasions." This is not necessarily bad, unless it indicated an unreadiness of mine to accept his feeling when it involves a dim view of the tuba.

He may go on after a while, "Collect, collect—that's all she wants to do, and I can't stand it. Antiques, matchboxes, old letters, even stamps." If my son has been pestering me for the money to buy an especially motheaten specimen of stamp, I may even fall a bit into my parishioner's mood of disparaging collecting. And so on.

Things of this sort are fairly obvious once looked at. And anyone who has done counseling in which he was able to concentrate single-mindedly on the parishioner's feelings and attitudes knows how fruitful this can be and is not so likely to let his personal interest divert him from it even when they are touched. But there is no counselor who does not at some times let himself be diverted to externals, especially when in more informal types of pre-counseling personal work.

The discussion of Alan with Chester is instructive

for the light it throws on the tendency to become preoccupied with externals.

Alan was a theological student who met Chester at a social affair in the home of mutual friends. Chester was a young veteran. Alan and Chester found themselves alone, talked about weather, football, and other matters of general interest. Chester had learned that Alan was a theological student although this had not previously come into the discussion. Then the following:

CHESTER: So you're studying to be a preacher? Well, I don't know about this religion business.

Alan, identifying himself with religion, feels his hackles rising. However, he spars for time:

ALAN: What do you mean, you don't know?
CHESTER: Well, how do you know what's right? Who gives you the authority to go around chastising people and insisting that they act this way or that?
ALAN: Have you met ministers who go around moralizing to you?

This is a defensive reaction of the "Name two" variety, when someone says he knows hundreds who are for what we are against or against what we are for.

CHESTER: Why, they all do. They act as if they have all the answers, as if they can pass laws for every individual. How can they be so sure that hard, rigid rules are right for every person?
ALAN: Has any minister ever told you anything that you didn't think was right for you?

CHESTER: Well—it's not that exactly. It's just that I've discovered some things that make me wonder about whether religion is right. Religion insists upon a certain kind of conduct, and people go ahead and accept it blindly, and then—well, a person does some of the things that religion condemns, and he finds—well maybe religion wasn't so right after all. I mean—

By this time it should have been clear to Alan that Chester, although opening the discussion with a shoulder chip, really has something he wants to discuss, and since Alan has not openly called him wrong or crazy, Chester interprets Alan's response as more positive than negative.

ALAN: Have you found that you disagree with some of the moral rules of the church?

CHESTER: Sometimes I just don't know. You see, before the war came along, I was one of the goody-goody boys. I was very religious, just as my family was—still is, I mean—and I went ahead and tried to do all of the things that our religion teaches. I never questioned any of them. Sometimes I found them hard to follow. Lots of times I violated them, but I always accepted them as being right.

ALAN: We all find the moral rules difficult to follow sometimes. Did trying to follow them make you unhappy?

Here Alan is diverted to an external generalization and then asks Chester a direct question. All of this is unnessary.

CHESTER: Not until I went into the service. There I found a different world. I found men doings things that I would have never done. And, gosh—well, it never hurt them. I mean, the fellows got drunk a lot, and they went out and got a woman occasionally. At first I thought it was awful—but—well, they were good guys, guys who'd do anything for you in a pinch, guys who'd die with you. Well, pretty soon I started going out with the fellows, and I did some of all the things that they did, and—well, I don't feel any the worse for it.

ALAN: You did what you think is right?

This is pushing Chester, for these words change the tone of Chester's point although literally they render it. It would have been quite different if Alan had said, "You can't feel those things are always really wrong?" The idea is the same, but connotations and overtones would have been much closer to Chester.

CHESTER: Sure I did—well, in a way I did—I mean, well, this is what makes me wonder about religion. I felt bad about it at first, but after all I hadn't really hurt myself. I had a lot of fun with the fellows, and—

ALAN: So you began to wonder whether or not the moral rules of the church were right for you?

CHESTER: Yes, that's it. When I came back, I just didn't fit into the conventional pattern that I had left. Ever since, I've been wondering.

In spite of all the errors Allan has made, at this point he has an opportunity to recoup. Chester is now talking seriously about his "wondering"—about the conflict he feels inside. Alan might have said, "That is, you can't see going back to the old pattern, but you aren't sure what your new pattern ought to be?" If he had, the chances are that real counseling would have begun. But here is what actually happened:

ALAN: Well, how have you made out here at home? Have you continued the habits you picked up in the Army?

The chance is gone. Alan wants to know *what* happened, not how or why. He is like the fiction readers who want fast-paced action narratives with a minimum of character and setting.

CHESTER: The whole situation is different—you don't do things at home that you would do with a crowd of men. Here at home I've found things pretty rough—different. Most of my friends are in college, or they're married, and I've been left pretty much alone to make out wherever I could find companionship.
ALAN: Well, how do you feel about your habits now that you're in this new situation? Do you still drink and get a woman?

Alan is not only asking for the facts; he is probing after them. Chester has already told him that is not the point. But Alan has got fixed on the externals and is going to get the narrative or know the reason why.

CHESTER: The whole thing is different.
ALAN: What do you mean?
CHESTER: Well, I tried night school for a while, but I didn't get anything out of it. So I came home and got this job I have.
ALAN: Are you happy in it?

CHESTER: Oh, it's something to do. About a year ago I started going with a real cute little girl. A lot of the people around town talked about it—she was pretty young—but I didn't care. She was very nice.

ALAN: Do you still go with her?

CHESTER: No, I wish I did. She and I were really crazy about each other. We wanted to get married.

ALAN: How did your ideas about morality work with her?

By this time it is becoming clearer that Alan is not really paying attention to Chester at all—but only to "the facts" about Chester's behavior so they can be used to get Chester to admit something in the moral realm, chiefly about his sexual activities.

CHESTER: I don't know. We didn't talk about it. We had sex relations a number of times. We wanted to get married right away.

ALAN: What happened to your plans?

CHESTER: Well, things got awfully mixed up. While I was away in the Army I met another girl, and I had invited her to come and see me some time. You know how you do those things. She was fine at the time. Well, what do you know, one day she wrote and said she was coming. I didn't know what to do. I couldn't stop her, and we had been pretty deep at one time.

ALAN: What a problem!

We may mercifully close the interview at this point, although Alan did not. He continued to get the story, how the old girl had come to town and found out about the new girl, and the new girl was sore because of the old girl, with the result that they both left Chester standing on the curbstone. In Chester's words they were both "unreasonable." Alan continued to throw loaded questions, such as "Did you desire them for anything else besides sex?"

In writing about it Alan had this to say: "My purpose here was to help Chester see the contradiction in his beliefs. He believed that his newly acquired loose morality was not hurting him, and yet his life was confused because of the fact that he had not recognized the dangers in his loose actions. It became obvious as we talked that there was much more underneath the surface than simply confusion about sex morals. He was, I found out later, a chap of high intelligence who had never done well in school because of lack of interest. He had never been popular. He had probably started going with the young girl because his being older and a veteran would attract her. I wanted him to see the validity of Christian morals, and I think that out of the talk he carried away an incipient understanding about the value of the standards which he had once followed during his church days. I think that he had begun to see that his indiscriminate use of the girls had hurt them and himself even though during the talk he would not admit it."

This statement reveals a deep and curious inconsistency in Alan's attitude. He shows that, at least on writing up the contact, he realized that there was more to it than sex and that Chester's entire orientation to life was involved. There are few signs that he had seen this during the contact itself. But his last two words are revealing on the other side—"admit it." Even though he says he recognized that Chester had a total problem in life adjustment to consider, nevertheless Alan's real concern in talking with Chester was to get him to admit something. He muffed all the opportunities which Chester gave him to talk about his whole conflicting attitude toward life, including attitude toward sex. If Alan really wanted to help Chester toward a more Christian view of sex, to try to get him to admit it was precisely the way not to do it.

We need to account for two things in Alan: why he was so tenaciously interested in the details of Chester's sex life, and why he was so obtuse in not paying attention to Chester's life problem in Chester's terms. As to the first we may wonder how solidly grounded is Alan's own view of sex, and how Christian. There seems a good deal of repression in it which sneaks out in such ways as an undue interest in Chester's sex behavior justified by the moral goal of the interest. This is not pathological unless Alan equates his own feelings about sex with the Christian view of sex.

How could Alan so often miss the importance of what Chester was trying to communicate? Presumably because he was so preoccupied that he did not even perceive its meaning until afterward. And he was preoccupied chiefly because of the sex distortion. The mechanism through which the preoccupation worked—and produced the blindness toward the real Chester—was externalization—being caught up in narrative rather than character, "the facts" rather than feelings, Chester's acts rather than Chester's views and conflicts.

In this case it was the sex references which served both as the channel and—in the moral justification form —as the excuse for paying attention to externals instead of to Chester. Almost anything can be such a vehicle, provided it has for us the same kind of meaning which the sex references had for Alan. That is, any discrepancy between what we believe in our heads to be our views and what they really are underneath will serve as a kind of trap to throw us off the path and have us become preoccupied with externals.

This means that it is not a conscious interest of ours, fully known to us, which is likely to be touched so that we divert ourselves in the counseling process. It is an interest whose true nature we have not altogether come to terms with—and which therefore pushes all the more strongly for remaining unacknowledged in its true strength.

I have an acquaintance whom I like, in spite of everything, but speaking with him is an exhausting business. I am lucky to get out a sentence before he is invariably reminded of something in what I have said; and this must be traced meticulously to its source before he can either listen to me or speak to the point from which we started. If he merely seized the conversation and carried it down a line, he might be boring, but he would not be exhausting. It is the butterfly character of any social intercourse with him that makes him fatiguing.

My suspicion is that this is his way—certainly not a consciously contrived strategy—of gaining control of situations. The meticulous documentation of his narratives is consciously intended as a mark of respect for his listener. The broad, and often unusual, bits of knowledge with which the flights are garnished are also intended to be flattering. But these become the justification for making impossible a straight-line discussion. I am forced to wonder, therefore, whether his maneuvers to control the situation are not, in effect, a kind of confession that he sees such relationships as encounters if not battles, and that he cannot bear to lose. This may not be so in his case, but the process is not unfamiliar to the psychologist.

Any interest of ours with which we have not come to terms—be it positive or negative—can be the occasion for diverting our attention to externals in counseling or in precounseling pastoral work. Dressed up in a certain way (like the moral interest of Alan), it can also serve as the justification we give to ourselves for moving to externals—even if we know that this is not the way good counseling proceeds.

Externals can wreck counseling. Preoccupation can produce externalization. Unexamined interests can permit preoccupation. We can let the tuba and the postage stamps take care of themselves. We are acquainted with them. It is the interests of whose interest-character we are unsure which are the demons of the piece.

SHYNESS IN COUNSELING

*H*OW CAN THE PASTOR MAKE CONTACT WITH shy people so that if they need help they will feel free to seek it from him? In its full dimension this is a difficult question. For there are many kinds of shyness, and shyness may mean very different things to different people. In spite of this complexity there appears to be one basic point which relates especially to shy people, and one basic error which we pastors tend to make in dealing with them.

We may first examine a contact by a minister with a parishioner, what I have called a precounseling pastoral contact. Here not all the conditions of counseling itself are present. Charlotte is aware that there is a problem, senses that it has something to do with her, but does not realize that another person may help her with it by helping her to understand and clarify its nature. If she were so ready, it would be a counseling contact. As it is, the contact may determine whether Charlotte comes to realize that she can confess her need for help and appeal to the pastor for it.

38

A young assistant pastor of a suburban church was assigned to special duty with the young people. When he began work, shortly before the following contact took place, the senior minister spent several afternoons and evenings taking him around to the homes of as many of the young people as possible. Bonner, the young pastor, reports that this provided a very useful introduction to most of the active young people.

A brief call was made by the two ministers on Charlotte. Before the call the senior minister told Bonner that she was a little older than most of her church group, and that she felt out of place in it. She did not work or attend school, but spent most of her time helping around the house. She recently had had a long illness, the nature of which was not known. Charlotte felt obligated to attend the young people's meetings, the senior minister said, because her mother insisted on it.

Bonner's own general observations at the time of the introductory call seemed to check with these comments. He reported that she seemed to have an attitude of inadequacy and looked discouraged about life.

On a subsequent Sunday evening an opportunity came for Bonner to talk with Charlotte. She was sitting on the side lines while the other young people were busy elsewhere.

BONNER: I'm glad to see you came tonight, Charlotte. I hope you've been having a good time.
CHARLOTTE: Well, not too bad. I don't know. I don't get along too well with this group.

BONNER: You don't feel as if you are really a part of the group?

CHARLOTTE: No. You see, I'm out of school now, and don't have much in common with the other girls. I don't know what goes on any more.

BONNER: You feel rather left out of things?

CHARLOTTE: Yes. The other girls got jobs and things when they left school, but I haven't done anything.

BONNER: What would you like to do?

CHARLOTTE: Oh, I don't know. I'm not very good at anything. I like to draw and paint, but I know I could never make a go of it. Jobs are hard to get, and I'm not that good.

BONNER: Did you study art in high school?

CHARLOTTE: Yes, and I liked it better than everything else put together.

BONNER: What did your teacher think of your work?

CHARLOTTE: O.K., I guess. I got good enough marks all right. But so did the other girls, and they haven't tried to go into art.

BONNER: Do you think you would like to go on and study in that field?

CHARLOTTE: I would like to, but I just know I wouldn't get anywhere.

BONNER: You are afraid you couldn't make the grade?

CHARLOTTE: Yes, there's no use. I haven't got the money to go to school any more anyhow, and there's so much competition—well, I've just stopped thinking about it.

BONNER: Do you do any work on the side?

CHARLOTTE: I haven't done any for some time now.

BONNER: What do you like to do best?

CHARLOTTE: Painting, drawing—anything that's art.

BONNER: Have you done much with oils?

CHARLOTTE: Quite a lot (*pauses to blow her nose*). This cold is giving me a lot of trouble.

40

BONNER: That's too bad. I hope you get over it soon.

CHARLOTTE: I got it last week down here. The others were dancing, and I was sitting near the open window. I can't stand drafts.

BONNER: We'll have to remember not to open a window tonight. Would you like to get into the dancing tonight?

Up to this point the assumption of the pastor has been something like this: If I can get her talking about her major interest, perhaps she will become less shy personally. Although he has asked a good many questions, he has made several stabs at following her leads at the points where she expressed something besides discouragement. He has not, however, followed her leads on negative feelings, in her case on discouragement. He might have done so, for example, if he had said, instead of "Do you do any work on the side?" something like this, "That makes you feel it would be foolish for you to consider it?"

It is certainly true, as the students of Dale Carnegie have found out, that an attentive interest in another person's interest often draws him out. If he is an enthusiast about beetles and horse racing, an insurance man who can get him talking about beetles and horses may improve his chances for a sale—provided the prospect does not catch on to the trick, or provided the insurance man's interest is genuine.

But even where this works, we may note that the pastor's concern is somewhat different from the salesman's. If true to his pastoral purposes, the minister is not merely interested in a sale or its equivalent. He is concerned with the growth of the person. Getting the person talking, or acting, or buying, is good only under certain conditions, namely, if it contributes to growth.

The pastor's assumption cannot be considered all wrong. Charlotte is shy and discouraged. If it is possible to get her voluntarily and happily busy about her greatest potential interest, it would certainly help her growth. And if she can talk about that interest in a positive way, it may help her to get started on it. But in her case this does not seem to be true. Her shyness and discouragement are too overpowering. What she says about art is accompanied by statements that she can really do nothing about it. Having found his approach does not draw Charlotte out in a positive way, Bonner believes he must try something else. So he turns to the contemporary scene and asks about the dancing which will soon begin.

CHARLOTTE: I don't think so. I'm not much good at it.
BONNER: You would like to, but are afraid it wouldn't go very well if you tried? (*Here Bonner follows her lead very well.*)
CHARLOTTE: That's right. I'm too short to swing with those tall boys.
BONNER: You are afraid that being short will keep you from doing the dance right? (*He is still following her lead.*)
CHARLOTTE: Yes, it's really no use for me to try.

By this time Bonner is getting a little desperate. On the whole he has followed the rule book, but all he gets from Charlotte is further statements of discouragement and disparagement.

BONNER: (*noting some of the group who have just gone over to the piano*) How would you like to go over and join with the others in singing?
CHARLOTTE: I guess I'd rather not.

By this time Bonner's repertoire is exhausted. He has tried drawing her out on her interests and following her leads. So he thinks: If I can just get her doing something, anything, with the young people, it will be a positive value. He lights on the first such possible activity now going on, and suggests singing. Negative reply.

BONNER: I'm sure the others would like to have us.
CHARLOTTE: You go ahead. I'll listen.
BONNER: All right. But come on over if you want to.

This is certainly much better than if he had said, as some do in similar circumstances: "Come on. You don't want to be a wallflower, do you?" Even so, Charlotte replied:

CHARLOTTE: I haven't any voice.
BONNER: You don't think you can sing well enough?
CHARLOTTE: No. I can hardly sing at all.
BONNER: We aren't very good at it ourselves, you know.
CHARLOTTE: I'm even worse.
BONNER: (*Bonner feels defeated. There seems nothing else he can do.*) Well, if it's all right with you, I'll go on over.
CHARLOTTE: (*smiling*) Sure.

43

Here is the way Bonner himself evaluated the contact: "From the standpoint of results this was a total flop. Not only was her attitude toward herself and her situation left unchanged, but I did not even succeed in getting her to voice her feelings to any great extent so that she could look at them for herself and perhaps begin to understand why she feels as she does. I feel that my approach was not altogether at fault, but there were many mistakes. I first missed the boat when I said: 'What would you like to do?' Here I turned to the external situation rather than continuing to focus attention on her feeling about the situation. Throughout I seemed to be trying to force things on her, first a decision to go to art school, then to join in dancing, and finally to get up and sing.

"I feel that my approach at other times was the correct one. The only trouble was that each time I displayed an understanding of her feelings, and followed her lead, she just repeated the feeling she had expressed before, which left everything where we started. Most people tend to go on to something else, or some elaboration, once their feelings have been expressed and understood. But she stuck by her guns every time, as if my repetition of her feeling made it all the more firmly entrenched."

This is a thoughtful analysis by Bonner, containing a great deal of insight. In retrospect he distinguishes between the occasions when he followed leads and those in which he did not. But he is troubled because following leads did not seem to get anywhere. The contact is, he feels, a total flop.

The most interesting thing to us about Bonner's analysis is what he does not discuss, the legitimate goals of this contact with Charlotte in the light of her situation as disclosed in the contact. To put it more generally, he does not consider what are the dynamics of Charlotte's situation. This means that his evaluation is not necessarily relevant to the real situation in which Charlotte is.

Our information about Charlotte is not great, but it is sufficient to make some very probable inferences. We see her shyness, lack of self-affirmation, and conscious discouragement. We know she spends her days merely working around her mother's house. We strongly suspect that the decision to attend young people's meetings is on her mother's urging. Let us be imaginative on the basis of this knowledge.

In a middle-class suburban home Mother would not order Charlotte to go to church. Instead she would say something like this: "I do hope you're going to the meeting tonight, Charlotte. You're almost nineteen now, and you need to get along with other young people. And nice young people too, the kind that go to church." If Charlotte said she did not want to go, or did not feel well, Mother would say, in effect: "But you'd better try it, dear, for your own good. You don't just want to stay in the house all the time."

We are justified in inferring that if this goes on now it has been going on all of Charlotte's life. She has not been permitted to learn to call her ego her own. At any point in life where she has succeeded in something, we can imagine her mother saying: "There, dear, I knew that if you did it that way it would work out right." And if she failed: "Well, dear, I was afraid that if you did it that way, it would not work." The mother would no doubt be horrified if told she dominates her daughter. But in fact this is a much more effective method of achieving dominance than merely giving orders.

We may swing imaginatively to what might have happened if Charlotte, at the meeting, had danced or joined in the singing, and even had a reasonably good time doing so. Upon her return home, her mother would have asked: "What did you do tonight? Did you have a good time?" And Charlotte would have had to answer, in effect: "I danced and sang. And you were right, Mother. I did have a good time." Mother's dominance, knowing best, would have been still more deeply embedded.

But Charlotte did not dance or sing. So when her mother does ask her the question when she arrives home, Charlotte can say: "Oh, the other kids danced and sang. But I just sat and watched them." At the price of not enjoying herself at the church Charlotte has, in a fashion, proved her mother wrong, given some resistance to the dominance.

We begin to see that the one positive growth point now evident in Charlotte is, strangely enough, not joining in activities and enjoying herself. This represents the one way in which, at this time, she is able to assert her selfhood. True, it is a negative way and in a sense self-defeating. But it is the sole way apparently open to Charlotte at this time. Her potential strength lies, therefore, in ability to refuse participation!

When this interpretation was suggested to Bonner, his first reaction was of shock and amazement. If this is true, he said, what good would it do to get Charlotte dancing or singing, or even painting? The answer was: No good at all, unless it was somehow done as an expression of Charlotte's self-affirmation and not—as it now would be —as a further proof that Mother always knows best.

But this means that Bonner's work, in the actual contact with Charlotte, was much better than he judged it to be. Unlike Mother, he did not press Charlotte to a decision to dance or sing or paint, for her own good. He could hear with some understanding her feelings of discouragement and to some extent draw her out on them without being under the compulsion to tell her to snap out of it.

The net effect of the contact was to create some confidence in him on Charlotte's part. She has come one step closer to readiness for the counseling she needs. But not understanding the dynamics of the situation, the pastor has judged his effectiveness to be much less than it really was. He has established a relationship in which patient follow-up becomes more likely to have some chance. But ignorant of the dynamics, he believes only that he has failed.

He believes that his following Charlotte's leads has not worked because she simply restated the same feeling. He has not seen that to state the other side of the feeling

—having some wish to sing, for instance—would make it inevitable in this situation that she would have to sing. That is, there is a dynamic reason why Charlotte does not move on to a positive attitude toward dancing or singing or art. From her standpoint these things are not at this time positive. Participation in them would not be strength, but capitulation.

There is one basic point that needs to be remembered in dealing with all shy people. This is, simply stated, that they are shy for some reason, that the shyness performs some function in their lives. Even if that function appears on the surface to be self-defeating, as in Charlotte—keeping her out of dancing, singing, and art school—it also reveals some kind of positive thrust—in Charlotte's case a blind attempt to maintain at least some sense of self-affirmation.

Any attempt, therefore, merely to brush away shyness, without perception into what it may mean to the person, may do more harm than good. There is one basic error that pastors tend to make in dealing with shy people. This is assuming that getting them into activity is necessarily a good thing. In Charlotte we see this is not so. Had the pastor been clever enough to get Charlotte dancing or singing, he would have been tempted to evaluate the contact as successful. Yet he would, in effect, have been aligning himself with Charlotte's mother, assuring her that Mother and pastor know best, and her own poor self has no self-starter.

This is not a word against the therapeutic values of fellowship. If Charlotte had been able to participate, because *she* wanted to and affirmed it for herself, in activities of the group, it would have been immensely helpful to her. If she had been in some kind of group therapy or group counseling session, in which the members told a little something of their own attitudes, it might have been very helpful, because it would have changed the meaning of activity participation at its roots. But so long as that meaning for Charlotte is one of knuckling down to Mother, and not affirming herself, it will not be useful to her. A special fellowship, such as a counseling relationship, is needed first.

Runners of program as we are, we pastors are sorely tempted to assume that participation in activity is good in itself, provided the activity is good and useful. But this, as Charlotte suggests, is not enough. The activity may be good, and the person may participate without compulsion at gun point. But if the meaning of that participation is not inwardly liberating to him, if he is not doing it with true voluntariness from the inside, it may not be a good thing.

The original question was: How can the pastor make contact with shy people so that, if they need help, they will feel free to seek it from him? Bonner has given more of the answer to this than he realized. We can follow leads, especially when they express negative feelings. We can express genuine interest and understanding without being overcome by any vested interest in keeping group activity going. We can avoid coercion even of a subtle variety. And we can then be patient, knowing that, having done this, we need to await the action of the Holy Spirit in making the person ready to seek help if he needs it. We can make ourselves geographically accessible. Bonner could have sought out Charlotte in a very short time. But he would still have been patient, and considered a small gain as of great significance, if it really showed a bit of self-affirmation on Charlotte's part.

Like Bonner, we do well to realize that part of the difficulty lies not in understanding Charlotte, important as that is, but in understanding what prevents us from seeing the Charlottes of our congregations as they really are. As with most pastoral counseling, personal insight can come as a by-product of effective reflection on our successes and our failures.

KNOWLEDGE IN COUNSELING

*J*s IT NECESSARY FOR THE PASTOR TO KNOW more than the parishioner in order to help him? If topics arise about which the pastor knows little, will the counseling relationship be impeded? What is the function of specific knowledge in counseling?

We may concede at the outset that there is one kind of knowledge about which the pastor should be very certain, whether the parishioner is or not. That is knowledge about the nature of counseling itself. If the pastor is unsure about what process must be gone through in order to help the parishioner move toward clarification of his difficulties, he will not succeed in doing effective counseling.

Our question relates to knowledge of content, not to knowledge of counseling process. If a parishioner is worried about whether cancer is hereditary, is it necessary or is it helpful for the pastor to be up on the best information about that subject? If a youngster wants to talk over possible colleges at which to enroll, is it necessary for the pastor to have this information? If a parishioner is troubled over the true meaning of the doctrine of original sin, how vital a part does the pastor's knowledge of that play in the counseling process?

Common sense can say a good deal that is valuable in reply to this question. There are occasions when almost any bit of sound knowledge which a pastor has can be put to good use. Since, as the philosophers say, all knowledge is one, the pastor may well be able to understand the true meaning of the parishioner in the light of some bit of knowledge, when otherwise he might remain in the dark.

Good sense suggests that further knowledge on the pastor's part may at times have value even if nothing emerges verbally from him. Take the cancer question, for instance. He may never state that cancer is, so far as is known, not hereditary. Yet that knowledge may enable him more easily to help the parishioner move toward an understanding of why this particular fear has pursued him.

But some aspects of the question go beyond common sense. They are well illustrated in the interview report which an advanced theological student, George, wrote about an informal contact he had with Beth, a senior high school girl in the church young people's group watched over by George. This group had been devoting several recent meetings to a study of various religious faiths. Beth had participated in this program and was believed by George to be especially able for her age and a diligent student.

On a Sunday morning George arrived at church a little early and went into the sanctuary to sit quietly for a few minutes before the service should begin. Beth came in a moment later and sat down beside George.

GEORGE: (*Not realizing she wished to carry on a conversation, I did not suggest we leave the sanctuary, and yet I found it difficult to carry on a conversation for breach of reverence.*) It would help us all if we would pause from the rush of things to think and meditate once in a while. (*I opened my worship bulletin and found the first hymn in the hymnal. After a moment I opened the conversation myself unthinkingly with a time-worn question.*) How is school?

BETH: Oh, fine. We have two weeks' vacation now, and am I glad. You see, I wrote a term paper for English class on Samuel Butler, which just about wore me out.

GEORGE: (*Not knowing much about Samuel Butler, I tried to avoid further display of my ignorance.*) Did you choose him as your topic, or was he assigned to the class as a whole?

BETH: Oh, I chose him, but I'm a little sorry now. I read fifteen books, and that's pretty hard to condense into twelve pages, and that was our limit. I don't know what to think about some of his ideas on religion. Maybe you can tell me how to answer his ideas about Christ's resurrection.

GEORGE: (*Saved by the bell! The organ began to play for the processional.*) Let's talk about it after the service.

After the service George and Beth went out together, and Beth opened the conversation. The minister's sermon had been on the subject "Is Religion a Gamble?" George described it as not a soothing sermon, mostly negative, time having run out just when the preacher was about to give his positive conclusions.

BETH: Butler seems to think religion is a gamble too. He says it can't hurt anyone to believe something, but that it might not be true either.

GEORGE: (*I inwardly questioned the authority of her remarks but assumed she wanted a starting place for conversation.*) Do you think Dr. Jones (*the minister*) thinks religion is a gamble? I thought he meant that only in a sense was religion a gamble, but that in another it was the only real thing.

BETH: No, I didn't mean that Dr. Jones is a skeptic. I guess I'm just confused this morning.

GEORGE: You mentioned his ideas about the resurrection. I must confess I don't know much about Butler. Most of his writings were novels, weren't they?

BETH: Yes, he was for the most part a novelist. (*She then recited in detail an account of his life and works, naturally taking a woman's delight in being able to tell a man something which he didn't know.*) But he also wrote about religion.

GEORGE: Just because he wrote about religion doesn't necessarily make him an authority, do you think? What in general that he said bothers you?

BETH: Well, our church believes in the resurrection of Jesus, doesn't it?

GEORGE: (*realizing that any detailed answer would be useless at the moment, I said*) Yes, it does.

BETH: Butler thinks it possible that Jesus didn't die at all, but that he just appeared to die, and that he later was seen by his disciples. I'm just mixed up. He presents his view so convincingly!

GEORGE: (*I could see the conversation had to be concluded soon. Another engagement called so that it was necessary to pre-*

pare. I gathered my coat.) I imagine Butler was one of the many skeptics of his time, who like some of the great German philosophers and theologians began to deny that Christ was divine. It's possible to prove almost anything you wish, you know, if you want to badly enough. Most modern scholars reject such teachings now; so I wouldn't worry too much about it. Of course, I do believe we should study all viewpoints, and often we can be strengthened in our own beliefs when we read about those which are different from our own. Are you coming to the meeting tonight?

BETH: Yes, I plan to be there.

GEORGE: Two weeks from tonight we're having a meeting entitled "What Do We Believe?" I will be acting as discussion leader, and I wonder if you would be willing to tell us a little about Butler's ideas as you have studied them. Perhaps you will be able to find some weaknesses in his arguments, and all of us would benefit by the discussion, I'm sure. Other members of the group, Nancy and Joe, will be sharing their ideas too.

BETH: That sounds good! I'd like to do it. If it's all right I'll bring this book along and quote a few passages. Of course I don't believe what he says, and it will be fun to argue against him.

GEORGE: Fine, Beth. Call on me if I can be of any help to you. Good-by.

Looking this over after he had written it up, George had some second thoughts. Here is what he wrote: "I naturally was anxious to help Beth keep her faith. It was obvious from the outset that she was deeply troubled by her reading and yet in a way flattered by the fact that she was bringing her own intelligence to bear upon her religious beliefs. I hoped that she might not take my word regarding the problem, but that she would think the matter out for herself. Actually, I was unprepared then and am now to deal intelligently with Samuel Butler. If I had more knowledge of his thinking with regard to religion, I might have taken a slightly different approach. Yet I feel it is best for her to work out the problem as far as she is able by herself. The later meeting in which she will take part may present a better opportunity for a direct exchange of information.

"In general I believe I used the only approach open to me at the time. Certainly there are many possibilities for the improvement of techniques. I know that I phrased many of my ideas poorly to her and that I probably offered too many direct suggestions to her in my closing remarks. Beth is now prepared to open an offensive against the problem which troubled her, and is no longer on the defensive."

In spite of the traces of self-criticism which George employs he is somewhat more sanguine about what happened than we may be. He believes his concluding remarks were too direct, but he suggests no insight into why he was impelled to make them. He hints that there is virtue in his having refrained from saying, "Beth, you just forget this Samuel Butler stuff and stick to Christianity." So far as that goes it is a virtue. He believes also that his reference to the later group meeting, inviting Beth especially to participate, keeps the situation open. In so far as this means Beth should feel free to discuss Butler then, George is right.

And yet, although his reflection on this contact has taught him something, it has not brought George far enough to see what was fundamentally wrong about his approach to Beth. This lies in his attitude toward his own ignorance of the content of knowledge involved, namely, Samuel Butler.

George had written, "Not knowing much about Samuel Butler, I tried to avoid further display of my ignorance. . . . Saved by the bell. . . . If I had had more knowledge of his thinking with regard to religion, I might have taken a slightly different approach." From George's point of view, he comes out squarely with an admission of his ignorance about Butler.

The fact is, however, that George's attitude toward his own ignorance about Butler is what rules this contact. In his head he admits his ignorance, and even does so verbally. But it is as if he then said to himself unconsciously: "Beth has no right to bring up something which I ought to know about and don't." There is more than a hint of this in his comment, "She then recited in detail an account of his life and works, naturally taking a woman's delight in being able to tell a man something which he didn't know."

Let us suppose that George had known a good deal about Butler. It seems likely that he would then have followed one of two courses. He might have said to her in effect, "But that isn't the way I understand Butler." Or, "Of course Butler is now discredited." As a matter of fact he does follow the second alternative so far as is possible without a knowledge of Butler. Had he specific knowledge, he would no doubt have done so more strongly.

This means that the more knowledge he had of Butler, the more firmly he would have tried to set aside Beth's attraction to that sparkling thinker. But in that case the function of his knowledge would have been corrective of Beth, not clarifying within Beth. It would have been used to show her more effectively that one side of her conflict *should* be out of account, and not to help her clarify for herself what the meaning *is* to her of the attraction toward Butler. The statements by George that he wants Beth to work this out for herself are meaningless in the face of this. They simply suggest the great distance that lies between his conscious intention and his actual motive.

We arrive, then, at the paradoxical conclusion that concentration on ignorance ruined this contact, but more knowledge would have made it worse! Plainly the difficulty cannot be in the knowledge or ignorance in themselves, but in attitude toward them. In this light the paradox begins to straighten out.

Our question then becomes: What do knowledge and ignorance mean to George? Our data are not complete enough to make us certain. But they suggest something like the following: Knowledge to George apparently means a buttress, a defense against being taken advantage of, an assurance to himself that he is worth something.

To be asked a question, and to know the answer, reinforces a sagging sense of self-esteem. To be asked a question, however, and be ignorant of the answer, is to depress further the self-respect. Although this may be compensated for in a measure by taking moral satisfaction out of admitting one's ignorance, it does not prevent George from showing thinly disguised hostility toward one who dares to force him to display his ignorance.

Knowledge for George, therefore, is in some way an instrument which takes the place of genuine mutual feeling in interpersonal relationships. It is not instrumental to those relationships but a kind of substitute for them. Even though George knows a little something about counseling, this makes his counseling knowledge of no value, because it affects his judgment at a level beneath that of his understanding of counseling.

This means that knowledge and ignorance mean something to George which has nothing to do with any particular knowledge or with the function of knowledge in general. Whatever the specific things in George's life which would account for the distortion, this bias exists, and exists at such a level that George remains unaware of it as a bias. He cannot perceive that knowledge and ignorance may have a different kind of meaning.

Our analysis of George could lead us into philosophical and theological as well as psychological channels. Philosophically speaking, all knowledge is abstract, that is, it is abstracted out of the concrete welter of events. Any time we forget this and attempt to treat the knowledge as if it were the concrete event, we go off the track. Theologically speaking, we get a hint about knowledge which is "existential" as against that which is not. George might pile up knowledge of a thousand Samuel Butlers, and yet he would get nowhere until he examined the meaning to him of knowledge and of ignorance.

The counseling moral of this story would seem to be that it is less a question of knowledge or ignorance than of what knowledge or ignorance means to the pastor. If it had been necessary for George to use knowledge as a substitute for something else, then to have some knowledge of Samuel Butler would have aided him in helping Beth. But in that case his ignorance of Butler in particular would not necessarily have stood in the way of helping.

We began by asking whether it is necessary for the pastor to know more than the parishioner in order to help him. We cannot reply that it makes no difference whether he knows more or less. But we can say that this is a very minor and subsidiary question in contrast to: What does knowledge or ignorance of something mean or symbolize to the pastor?

If knowing means to us, inwardly, being worth while, and not knowing means being exposed or rendered defenseless, then in counseling we shall be compelled to defend our ignorance and attack with our knowledge— in which case we shall be ignoring the first essential of counseling, concentration on understanding the parishioner.

If knowing, on the other hand, means something positive, an inward expression of our distinctively human strength, and ignorance means a stimulus, not a threat, then we may use our knowledge, remain unembarrassed by our ignorance, and continue concentrating on the person we are trying to help.

Surely it is not unnatural that knowledge should acquire a distorted meaning for so many persons of education and sensitivity. For the most part the matrix in which our knowledge has been acquired has been highly competitive, a spelling bee writ large over the pages of the sciences and the humanities. We have learned the lesson that knowledge is instrumental, but there tends to be a serious discrepancy between our heads and our viscera when we try to answer: Instrumental for what?

Any such distortions which exist come into sharp focus in pastoral counseling. Conversely, any true insights into the meaning and function of knowledge can help our counseling. There is no better way to put a distorted meaning of knowledge in its place than to experience the satisfactions derived from practice on the basis of a true meaning of knowledge.

FLEXIBILITY IN COUNSELING

*A*LL TOO EASILY DO OUR COUNSELING MINDS resort to rigidities. A principle or procedure which we have found widely applicable becomes a rigid dogma or rite, and we then apply it where it has no relevance.

There is no recipe for the maintenance of flexibility in counseling except perhaps concentration on the parishioner. But there is a valuable aid to this in the form of compelling ourselves to come clean with ourselves about our current interpretation of the counseling situation. If we rest in the illusion that we are open-minded and therefore have no interpretation, at least until the job is finished, what usually happens is that an unreflective interpretation creeps in against our knowledge.

When first teaching theological students to put life histories together in a mental hospital, I found the most difficult thing for them was learning to separate fact from interpretation. I insisted that they write separate sections, the first as objective an account as possible of the stages in the life of a patient which had led up to his illness, and the second a come-clean, telling why they really believed this happened. The distinction between fact and interpretation is far from a final one; yet a clear practical line of demarcation can be drawn. The students preferred to put the sections all together without distinction. When that happened, it proved difficult to help a student see a correction even of facts about the life history, for these were so firmly wedded to an interpretation which he had nevertheless not pulled out and examined as an interpretation. When he had mastered the practical distinction, education proceeded much more smoothly.

The question of interpretation in counseling is usually about what shall be suggested as interpretation to the parishioner. We are not here concerned with that. We are asking instead what interpretation the pastor gives to himself—in our conviction that he has one anyhow whether he is aware of it or not, and that if he comes clean to himself about it as an interpretation he will retain more flexibility in his counseling. His tentative feeling about the whole situation may still be vague. If so, there is some value in admitting that. But if he tries to push down his current interpretation on the ground that he does not have enough facts or wants to avoid prejudging, he is in much greater danger of falling into rigidity. It is good for one's professional soul to have interpretations, acknowledge them, and form the practice of discarding them when new light shows their inadequacy.

The distinction is similar to that which a great educator, Elliott Dunlap Smith, notes between the outlook of the pure scientist and that of the professional man. The scientist seeks new knowledge, but he seeks to explore it within certain channels which he has arbitrarily made narrow. When he discovers something, then he tests its application; if it does not fit the problem to which he has applied it, his concern is to try it on something else. In contrast the professional man begins with the problem and seeks knowledge from here and there, exact or inexact, which will come closest to helping him answer it. Of course both types are needed, and each can become a victim of its own form of rigidity. But the professional man—who may also be a scientist but who is professional because his concern begins with patient or client or parishioner—is impelled again and again by his professional responsibility to move away from the rigidity of past practice and to explore new possibilities and new combinations. So far as he is genuinely professional and not just the exerciser of a trade, it is his flexibility which makes him so.

An interesting illustration of flexibility in a counseling situation has come from James Tracy, a theological student who is a boys' club leader as a part of his field work training. Inexperienced as Mr. Tracy was in counseling, he chose well when in a situation in which flexibility proved effective and in which adherence to an original plan would have spelled failure. While his knowledge of counseling was not large at the time of this contact, it was well integrated; and he came clean with himself on what he had. The result is a surprisingly effective bit of counseling.

Mr. Tracy became concerned about one of the boys in his club, Merle "Skip" Murdock. Skip was physically smaller and weaker than any other boy, although a bit older than most of the others. Skip tried continually to attract attention to himself in meetings, often saying anything that came into his head whether it made sense even to him. The other boys picked on him all the time, and Skip could never take it. All this concerned Mr. Tracy.

Upon inquiry Mr. Tracy learned that Skip and his father were not close, and the family affairs seemed to be run by Mother. It occurred to Mr. Tracy that Skip might be, as he put it, "starved for companionship, especially male." Telling himself forthrightly this interpretation, he telephoned Skip's mother one day and made an appointment to come talk with her. After his arrival there was weather talk, and then the following ensued.

TRACY: I've been a little concerned about Skip, Mrs. Murdock. He doesn't seem to fit in too well with the other fellows in the club.

MRS. MURDOCK: How do you mean (*a little worried*)?

TRACY: Well, whenever the fellows pick on someone, it's always Skip.

MRS. MURDOCK: Yes, I know he doesn't get along too well. He often comes home almost crying and tells me how they have tormented him, and made him miss his bus home, and everything. If he could only get along better with them! But he is such a tease that it does get rather annoying at times. You can hardly blame the others, especially when they find out that Skip just can't take being teased or picked on himself.

TRACY: Then at least some of the trouble he brings upon himself?

We may pause to note how effective is Mr. Tracy's opening of this contact. He defines the situation forthrightly. He does not beat about the bush trying to reassure her anxiety prematurely, saying it may not be Skip's fault. The result is that Mrs. Murdock is able to discuss it forthrightly also.

MRS. MURDOCK: Yes (*pause*). He used to be such a nice boy, just a darling, until he was four years old. Then he became ill.

Mrs. Murdock then described how Skip had been stricken with several diseases at once, including one which left him for a long period unable to move his arms. During a convalescent period it had been necessary for his mother to wait on him hand and foot. He finally recovered but has been physically fragile ever since.

MRS. MURDOCK: I had to spoil him to save his life at all. Now he is all right, but he's weak and can't fight back like a boy should be able to do. He doesn't do well in school, but he's not stupid. He can do very well when he wants to. He's not a bad boy. He always tells the truth, and never does anything seriously bad. But it's his constant teasing.

At this point Mrs. Murdock paused. During the long recital she was restrained but obviously moved. At the end the tears almost became open crying. She smiled, and then:

MRS. MURDOCK: All this time he's been my chief worry, that boy.

TRACY: You've been *very* much concerned about this whole thing.

This is perhaps the turning point of the interview. We may recall that, before the call, Mr. Tracy had suspected the difficulty as coming from Skip's being mother-dominated and having too little contact with his father. In any event he had come to talk about Skip—not to do counseling with Mr. or Mrs. Murdock. In reply to Mrs. Murdock's long story about Skip's illnesses it would have been very understandable if he had said, "Skip certainly did have a hard time in his earlier years," or "I've always suspected there must have been something like that in the background." But what Mrs. Murdock has been expressing is not just the narrative of Skip's illnesses but her own feelings about this process. Because he has tagged and admitted the interpretation he had before he arrived, Mr. Tracy is able to set it aside and look squarely at the feelings Mrs. Murdock has been expressing. From this point on he is counseling with Mrs. Murdock—in a limited area, to be sure—but definitely with *her,* and not just with Skip through her.

MRS. MURDOCK: Yes. Sometimes I just don't know what to do. He's so lonely. He hasn't any friends at all. He comes home right after school, and there aren't any kids his age in the neighborhood. He has a bike, and he just got a pair of skates, but he wants to spend all his time indoors by himself. That's not right for a boy! He ought to be outside playing. He ought to have one good friend, and be friends with several others.

TRACY: If he had just one close friend, the fellowship would help a lot.

MRS. MURDOCK: I've tried every way I could to get him into groups where he could make friends, but his annoying behavior always causes trouble. Last week he was thrown out of the after-school pottery class. You know he's good at that. He likes it a lot. In fact it's the only thing he'll go to without my pushing him.

TRACY: He *can* do well at the things he likes to do? (*pause during which Mrs. Murdock makes no comment*) You've tried everything you could think of?

Mrs. Murdock has tried everything she can think of. She would like someone to suggest some other action which can be tried. While this is not likely to help, it is not an easy temptation to resist. Also, when Mr. Tracy reflects her feelings in his last comment above and gets no reply, he might easily have turned and asked her if she had any suggestions about how he should treat Skip in the club. This would not have proved fruitful. Instead he must have asked himself, "What basically has she been trying to communicate to me since I got here—why, the fact that she's tried everything and feels bad because nothing has worked." So his words are a kind of summary of her central theme.

MRS. MURDOCK: He's been my main concern all these years. At times I feel that I don't know what to do. (*pause and a sigh*) It's been very hard.

TRACY: It *has* been hard for you.

MRS. MURDOCK: (*after a pause*) His father hasn't understood the boy. Since his sickness he has hardly spoken to his son. I've tried to explain time and again that Skip especially needs his father. But he said I was trying to push the child off on him.

Mr. Tracy's willingness to "wait it out" has borne fruit. It is with hesitation that the father is brought in, but this does happen.

TRACY: If he had had the fellowship with his father, it would have helped tremendously?

MRS. MURDOCK: Oh yes! But his father just didn't understand. His father does pottery, you know. Skip would ask him about tools and materials and things while he worked on it in the basement, but his father would just turn away and not even answer the child. All these years when he especially needed the companionship of his father he didn't have it.

What Mrs. Murdock has now stated is almost precisely the interpretation which Mr. Tracy had had before the call. But in the meantime he has been doing his best to look at the situation through Mrs. Murdock's eyes, with the result that the earlier interpretation, while perhaps having truth in it, is nevertheless inadequate.

At this point Mrs. Murdock excused herself and walked quickly out of the room. In a minute she returned with a handkerchief in her hand. She began to talk as she walked across the room to reach her chair.

MRS. MURDOCK: They get along all right, Skip and his brother. Joe is nice to him as long as Skip behaves himself. But if he starts to tease, Joe just won't stand it. So Skip really hasn't anyone to depend on but me.

TRACY: You've had to carry on by yourself all this time.

MRS. MURDOCK: Well, his father is finally coming to understand and is helping him now. And he has a very good teacher in school now. He *has* shown some improvement.

TRACY: He is showing improvement, then?

MRS. MURDOCK: Oh yes, he has definitely improved some, but he has such a long way to go (*wearily*).

TRACY: Though it's still bad, there *is* hope.

MRS. MURDOCK: Yes, I'll just keep trying. It certainly was nice of you to come to talk with me about this.

TRACY: Well, I'd like to help Skip, Mrs. Murdock, and I'll try to do anything I can to help him straighten out.

The last part of this is the most mechanical and insecure of all, and Mr. Tracy plainly missed some good chances. By this time his inexperience has hit him too forcibly, and he fears he has got into deeper water than he had counted on. The errors, however, are not serious enough to undo the clarification which he has helped Mrs. Murdock to get.

There are several subtleties about this contact which Mr. Tracy never saw at all. He did not see Mrs. Murdock's self-blame and her attempt to shift it. He apparently did not see how wanton had been the father's misunderstanding. He did not assess at full value Mrs. Murdock's confidence in him as judged by what she told him. He did not see how inwardly torn she was, not just about what to do for Skip, but also about her feelings toward Skip.

In addition it is to be doubted whether his interpretation at the end of the call was substantially better than that at the beginning. He wrote, for instance: "Her problem is her boy, and not so much her attitudes and emotions about the boy." It is true there is a problem as to what action to take about the boy. But Mrs. Murdock's own feelings toward Skip and toward her husband about Skip are in considerable confusion.

In spite of these mistakes and oversights Mr. Tracy was able to do what was—for an inexperienced theological student—a phenomenal job of helping. The reason lies in his flexibility. He came to talk about Skip. Instead she wanted to discuss her feelings toward Skip. He wanted to get some action, especially on the part of the father. Instead she wanted understanding about the difficulties of effective action. Yet when these things came, he changed his plan, was alert to what she tried to communicate, and therefore helped.

It would be difficult to analyze what lay behind Mr. Tracy's capacity to be flexible without going into his personal life. No doubt his knowledge of counseling helped. Probably his not being an overaggressive person was also important. But the chief thing seems to be that he could be flexible and concentrate on what was really there, because he had acknowledged to himself his interpretation before he went, but in a spirit which could allow him to change rather than hang on to it. It was, in a real sense, only a hypothesis. But because it was clear to him, he could discard it as soon as it proved inadequate. The fact that his later interpretation was not much better did not vitiate the relative success of the counseling.

The point seems to be, then, to hold interpretations at any stage as hypotheses, tentatively, and to take away any tendency we have to defend them by coming clean to ourselves about them at every step of the process. What this does is to break down what might otherwise become rigid, so that we can, within the limits of our insight, concentrate on the person we try to help. Where our knowledge is as small as Mr. Tracy's, we may help only a little. But even if it is as small as his, we do really help when we are able to move in the direction he did.

Do we, the counselors, have goals in counseling? I believe we inevitably have them. If I think it important enough to make a call on Mr. Henry, whose wife was buried two days ago, I have something in mind, however vague. While it would hardly be in order to say to myself, "I'm going to make him talk to me about his wife whether he wants to or not," it is a goal if I believe that it may be better if he can talk to me than if he cannot. But when I arrive, and find perhaps that he will not touch the subject of his wife at all, or will not even see me, I need not feel my larger purposes defeated. I simply have to readjust. If I have been clear with myself, that is not difficult. If I have concealed from myself, it may be very difficult.

It is impossible for us to be in a counseling situation for five minutes without forming certain impressions. These are not final interpretations, but they partake of the nature of interpretation. Instead of repressing these and saying to ourselves, "Here, I mustn't consider her an old witch quite as soon as this," or "Stop that! How can I be sure he's badly mistreated even if he does talk convincingly?" we can admit to ourselves that this is how it now strikes us. Like anything else in the psychic life that is acknowledged, it fails then to have the compulsive power of a repression. Because we have not identified our self-esteem with our interpretation, we have little difficulty in changing the latter.

Flexibility is certainly not chameleonism. It is not the absence of goals or theories or interpretations. Instead it is the willingness—within the broad theoretical framework—to be alert to unpredicted novelty in the situation which may alter our current interpretation. And confessing our current interpretations to ourselves is an important way to keep our counseling flexible.

CONCENTRATION IN COUNSELING

ONE OF THE EASIEST PRINCIPLES TO GRASP and the most difficult to apply in counseling is concentration. If we have examined counseling at all, we soon see that the cardinal sins are all opposites of concentration: diversion, coercion, moralization, and generalization. If a parishioner needs counseling, he has inner conflicts and tensions. If we, within the limits of the counseling situation, help him to get those out verbally so they can be examined at his own pace, we perform the essence of the counseling function. If we concentrate on what he is trying to communicate, this can happen.

But how difficult this is to apply! Mrs. Jones is working over the problems she has with her husband, and says suddenly, "You know, I think if I learned how to pray, all this would be easier." We forget to concentrate, and outline so many stages of prayer, or how someone else learned to pray, or what prayer means to us. Mrs. Jones is diverted. Instead of concentrating on whatever she means by it and letting her tell us, we react to the word "prayer" as Pavlov's dogs did to a bell.

74

Or we are doing fine concentrating on Mr. Smith's situation until he comes to his fear of homosexuality. He doesn't really think he's homosexual, he says, but he's had dreams, and certain sensations when in dressing rooms, that worry him. We turn to him and ask, "But have you ever had any real homosexual experience?" If the answer is yes, we are no longer considering the problem on the terms he felt inwardly able to use in presenting it; his anxiety is up, and the chances of our helping him are down. If the answer is no, we have diverted him from his fear, which actually does worry him, as if to say that all this is of no account unless he has had homosexual relations.

But it is doubtful, in such situations, whether we can say we understand the principle of concentration if we cannot apply it in practice. Even though the idea seems clear in our minds, the implications remain fuzzy. And a notion whose implications are blurred is not very clear. It may well be that the clarity we believe we have over the importance of concentration is partly illusory.

But the principle of concentration *is* right. It must be, then, that we do not have enough experience of its rightness to make that come clear in our minds on the occasions when our own inner tensions and needs push us away from using it.

The deep and simple power of concentration in counseling may be studied in an interview which Pastor Jardin had with Simonette. Jardin was a French minister who came to the United States for graduate study. While here

75

in a large city he arranged to make calls in a hospital upon French-speaking patients who did not otherwise have pastoral ministry. All he knew of Simonette before calling upon her was her name. She seemed to be in her early twenties.

JARDIN: Good morning. I am Pastor Jardin. Your name is Simone?

SIMONETTE: (*somewhat surprised at the unexpected visitor*) Yes, although at home they call me Simonette.

JARDIN: Then I must call you Simonette.

SIMONETTE: (*smiling*) Well, it is the same for me. As you know, our parents wish to call one by names which are meant for children. But when I was admitted to the hospital I gave my official name.

JARDIN: How are you feeling today?

SIMONETTE: Oh, I feel much better, thank you.

JARDIN: As I call at Blank Hospital in Paris, I am interested to visit the French who are in this hospital.

SIMONETTE: (*more freely and confidently*) I know that hospital. When I was about twelve years old, I was seen there twice. I am very grateful that you are so kind to come to see me. How long have you been here in the city?

JARDIN: Just a year, and will be going back next June.

SIMONETTE: (*looking thoughtful*) Oh—I wish I could get out of here and go home soon.

JARDIN: Do you feel that you are well enough to go home?

SIMONETTE: Well, I am much better now, and I think that I am well enough to go home. I have been here in bed for two months, and I am tired of the bed. Besides, everybody here speaks only English, and although I understand it quite well, I cannot speak it fluently enough. My only relative in this city is an aunt, and she cannot come to see me very often because she is working.

JARDIN: Have the doctors or nurses told you about when you may go home?

SIMONETTE: Well, they have not exactly, but it seems that it will not be very soon. (*She pauses.*) I had pneumonia, and they admitted me to this hospital. As a result of the pneumonia I have a cavity in a lung. And they tell me that they must send me to another hospital for some time. But I do not wish to go. I would like to go home. I feel that I will get completely well there.

JARDIN: You feel that you do not wish to go to another hospital and would rather go home?

SIMONETTE: Yes. But they tell me that I should have special treatment that I cannot have at home, and I do not know what to do (*said inquiringly*).

JARDIN: You have difficulty in deciding what to do. If you ask to be sent home where you would feel more happy, or go to the other hospital where you would have the special treatment you need for getting well—

SIMONETTE: That's right. And I think I am too sentimental about it.

JARDIN: You think you are too sentimental. What makes you think so?

SIMONETTE: Well, I have been thinking only about my being with my aunt, or going back to France where my parents live; but maybe I have not understood that the best for me is to go to the other hospital where I can get well. If I go back to France, I might get worse.

JARDIN: You think that going to the other hospital would be the best thing for you?

SIMONETTE: Yes. There I will get well soon. Don't you think so?

JARDIN: You said the doctors think it is necessary for your health.

SIMONETTE: That's right—and I think I should follow their advice. This conversation has helped me very much. Could you come to see me again? I will be in this hospital for about two weeks more.

JARDIN: I will be very glad to come again. I will come to the hospital again next Monday. What about that day?

SIMONETTE: I will be delighted. You have helped me greatly.

In his evaluation Pastor Jardin wrote: "I noticed that she felt free to speak and let her real problem come out. She seemed to be wanting to go home, but at the same time doubting if that was the best thing for her or whether she should go to the other hospital where she is to be sent. In trying to follow her leads and helping her to clarify I think I helped her. Of course I did not wish to mention to her the authority of the law which made it compulsory for her to go to that hospital instead of going home. I wished to help her express herself freely and then try to discover her problem and make her own decision. I feel that her statement as to the help she had received from my visit to her was a sincere one. She was brought to understand her situation and to decide for herself what was the best choice for her between the two conflicting ideas."

We must admit that the pastor opened this contact with a big advantage. Both he and Simonette were from a different country, and Simonette was lonely above all for someone from France. Yet this initial advantage might have been dissipated if the pastor had ridden through on a stereotype, French or American.

But what strikes us most forcibly is the astonishing result which the pastor got in such a short time. It is true that the contact was written up from memory, and more words were undoubtedly said than were placed on paper. Even so, the result seems almost miraculous. Simonette has tuberculosis. Without proper hospital care she cannot live. And without an affirmative attitude toward the rest which her treatment requires she may not get well. It is vital both to have the treatment and to take it with complete accord from inside her.

Yet she is lonely, homesick, and bored. Why is the hospital treatment so valuable? she asks herself. If it is all so hard on her, may she not be better off where her spirit feels good? We can see that there is a point in this. If she were where she could be happy—and still rest and get medical care—she would be better off than with the best medical care and a spirit of rebellion.

If Jardin had put on an arrogant bedside manner and told her that she must do this and stop being a baby, he might have got her to consent but without the inward affirmation which is not only essential to her feeling decent but also to her cure from tuberculosis. Even if he had done so subtly, the result would have been the same.

Jardin saw at once that he had an interest in getting her to the other hospital. But he had an equal interest in her deciding to go on her own. Therefore he was able to listen to her feelings on both sides without a sense of strain in his own attitude. His concentration on what she was trying to communicate was not difficult—because he sensed its point and meaning.

On due reflection we may well be convinced that Simonette had come very close to such a decision even before the pastor called on her. Yet the tiny difference might mean everything. We can imagine that the facts had been explained to her by doctor or nurse or social worker. But somehow it did not click in "her own language." She was almost persuaded, but this is different from making a decision oneself. To talk in her own language, both literally and figuratively, with someone who understood made a decisive difference.

Jardin made technical mistakes, leaned a bit hard on the side of medical authority, and might well have gone a bit further than he did. And yet none of these criticisms touches the essential point that an excellent job was done —and done because of his single-minded concentration.

There are many points where he might have done something ineffective. He might have been tempted to have reminiscent talk about France, or to ask whether other friends might come to see her, or to give his impressions of America. He did none of these things. In addition to his seeing the value of concentration we must also say about him that his own attitude did not stand in the way of such concentration. He did not have to sweat and struggle to keep such things down. He had genuine interest in Simonette and what she was struggling with.

As a matter of fact he was a person of unusual stability. Perhaps we may say that he was able to concentrate for two related reasons. His previous counseling experience had taught him the "feel" of concentrating and the surprising values that may often emerge from it; and his personal problems, whatever they might be, could be held sufficiently in perspective that they did not need to intrude unexpectedly into his pastoral activity. In him reason and emotion had got together.

It is possible that concentration can be the entering point for a beneficent circle, instead of a vicious circle, in counseling. Suppose that we have tried hard to learn counseling, that sometimes things seem to work and sometimes they don't, that we have become discouraged, for it all seems so complicated; even such a book as this, analyzing cases, mainly shows us what we have not thought of before. Our mood is discouragement.

At such a point it may be wise to keep the mind focused on just one thing—Are we concentrating on what this person is trying to tell us? Forget about technique, complications, everything else but concentrating. We may have to struggle a bit for it. But suppose, even though struggling and a bit tense, we really succeed; then of course from point to point we will naturally be clarifying to the other person what we have understood. If we miss it, he corrects us, and nothing is lost.

When this is done, an astonishing number of situations move in the direction of the Jardin-Simonette interview—not usually so far, but in a similar direction. This may occur even when we have had to pull in our ideological horns to keep from talking about our own childhood, or why brown eggs are better than white, or the evils of communist totalitarianism.

But getting this far means, within limits, successful counseling experience. We cannot only see something happening. We can also feel it ourselves. We have, however forcibly, begun to develop a habit of attention and concentration, and there is a sense of inner strength as a result of exercising it.

We have still not touched our specific hindrances to concentration. But those obstacles may be very much easier to face if we have achieved an inner feeling, based on some mildly successful experience, that this really does get results. If we have such a feeling, then we may begin to observe ourselves, as it were, in this situation where our heads know that concentration is called for but our emotions threaten to divert us.

If I develop an almost overpowering impulse to stop listening to a teen-ager talk about which college he is going to apply for, and give him the real dope, and I catch myself in the act, I may now be strong enough to be able to admit to myself that showing what I know, even just to myself, is something on which I rely for propping up self-esteem. Not a very pleasant insight. But if it is true, and if I avoid it, the tendency will pop out in repeated temptations to inject my knowledge where it has no relevance. If I take the pain of the insight, I become in some measure free from a compulsion.

If I can proceed in this fashion—consolidating a legitimate strength and using that new-found strength to stand on while examining a hitherto unexamined weakness—I am of course improving my counseling in large degree. And I may find some of the insights, both the painful and beneficent, relevant in other relationships as well.

Such a procedure cannot be the equivalent of personal psychotherapy. But I am convinced that the sound analysis of our own pastoral counseling, in this fashion, can affect favorably our personal attitudes. If those attitudes have been warped by past experience so that psychotherapy is necessary, then it should be had. But all pastors can learn from reflection on their pastoral counseling not only about their parishioners but also about themselves. Concentration seems a good point at which to start.

TIMING IN COUNSELING

Chapter Seven

O NE OF THE MOST IMPORTANT SENSITIVITIES
we need in counseling is timing. To paraphrase Ecclesi-
astes, there is a time to start and a time to stop; a time
to plant an idea and a time to wait and see if it grows;
a time to kill pretensions and a time to let them strangle
themselves; a time to analyze and a time to build up; a
time to emphasize interest and a time to be objective; a
time to help cast away the stones of old patterns and a
time to gather up other stones into new meaning; a time
to keep silence and a time to speak; a time to define the
situation forthrightly and a time to educe; a time to
understand negativities and a time to encourage the
emergence of creative powers.

Many things are obvious about timing in counseling.
For instance, when reactive emotion is high in response
to some loss situation which has just occurred, we cannot
have counseling in the same calm manner that might be
helpful and even essential some weeks later. Or when a
person is just arriving at the unpleasant discovery that
some of his difficulties are within him, we do not say the

same things to him as we would a little later, after he has absorbed this fact and resolved consciously to try to get help.

Many of the apparent controversies over directive versus nondirective counseling fade into minor issues when studied in the light of timing. One can reflect or mirror feelings to the parishioner's profit only after the latter has come to the point of seeing how this process may help him. Prior to that such a procedure would mean something quite different to him, perhaps cold-blooded detachment.

There are, however, subtleties about timing which lie in the attitude of the pastor as well as in the readiness of the parishioner or the character of the relationship between pastor and parishioner. They usually arise through stereotyped thinking about problems—reasoning from one valid instance to another which is taken to be similar but in fact is not. That is, they arise out of faulty generalizations. The insight we got in one situation may have been sound. But because we did not properly consider its setting, and its timing, we may then apply it inappropriately where it does not fit.

An excellent illustration of this faulty generalization about timing comes from the young pastor of a community church. Some weeks before the pastoral interview an older man in the parish became ill, and a surgical operation was attempted. The surgery disclosed that he had an inoperable cancer and had only a few days or weeks to live. The pastor was with the man's family when this word came from the surgeon. The pastor prayed with them.

During the eight weeks thereafter, while the man we shall call Mr. Perkins was hovering between life and death, the pastor called frequently on him, spoke briefly with him when he was conscious, and had prayer with him. Mr. Perkins was unaware that he had cancer and felt sure he was going to live. Well drugged, he suffered little pain.

Mrs. Perkins spent twelve hours a day at the hospital, and the pastor saw her there every day or two. Here is how he described this series of sessions: "My words with her varied with her mood. We faced frankly the fact of her husband's certain death. We talked about death, and life in the light of it. She asked me one day if it was a sin to pray for a miracle. I said that I did not think so. It seemed that the miracle she wanted was for her husband to be entirely cured. I did not discourage her in this, but I tried to make the miracle be related more to the happiness that she was knowing day by day as she sat by the bed of her husband. I prayed with her, comforted her, and put myself at her disposal."

The actual death of Mr. Perkins came suddenly two months after his illness was discovered. Death itself was not difficult. Immediately on receiving the news the pastor went to the home and spoke briefly with the grown-up Perkins children. Mrs. Perkins, exhausted, had gone to bed and was asleep. Next morning the pastor called again, and the following interview took place.

PASTOR: Hello. I'm awfully sorry.

MRS. PERKINS: Thank you. I did what I could.

PASTOR: I know you did.

MRS. PERKINS: Won't you sit down?

PASTOR: Yes. Thank you.

MRS. PERKINS: Well, there isn't much to say. I prayed that I could have him a while longer, and God gave me that. I'm thankful for that.

PASTOR: We're all thankful. You had your miracle, didn't you?

MRS. PERKINS: Yes, but I wish I could have had him longer.

PASTOR: So many people have spoken to me lately about the sorrow you've had these last few years: first the death of your daughter and now these many weeks of suffering. You've had some hard years.

MRS. PERKINS: Yes, but you have to accept it. I was bitter when Ann died, but I've come to accept it.

PASTOR: I'm so glad that Mr. Perkins was with you these last few days at home. He enjoyed himself, didn't he?

MRS. PERKINS: Yes, but he didn't feel right. He had those stomach attacks, and his mind went. But I'm thankful that he came home. He saw the tulips above ground that he planted last fall. That pleased him. But it was hard caring for him. I had a practical nurse come in, but she was no help at all. I knew as much as she did. I learned a lot at the hospital.

PASTOR: You learned to become a good nurse. But you're tired, aren't you?

MRS. PERKINS: Yes I am. I feel that I could sleep for weeks and weeks.

PASTOR: I hope that you'll take time to get a good rest.

MRS. PERKINS: You'll be able to be with us on Wednesday for the funeral?

PASTOR: Yes. I wonder if there is anything especially meaningful to you that I could include in the service. Anything from the Bible or from poetry? Anything that your family shared that you would like to have? I want this service to be entirely yours.

MRS. PERKINS: No, I don't think of anything offhand. May I let you know?

PASTOR: Certainly. I'll be down again before Wednesday. Are there any arrangements that I can help you with?

MRS. PERKINS: No, my children are being so helpful. They haven't left me alone since last night. Sue is sick again with flu, so we have to take care of her.

PASTOR: I hope that you won't become too tired during these next few days. You know, to tell you the truth, I was a little worried about you at first; but after seeing you stand up to the pressure of the last few weeks, I have real confidence in you.

MRS. PERKINS: Well, I was determined that I wasn't going to fold up.

PASTOR: Shall we pray together?

MRS. PERKINS: Yes, please.

PASTOR: Gracious God, our heavenly Father, we believe profoundly that thou art our God, that thou art very near to us. Thou dost guide us day by day, dost lift us up when we are fallen and in despair. Underneath are thine everlasting arms. We believe that by thy grace life is continued in thee. Strengthen us now in these days; keep our trust ever in thee. Support us all the day long of this troublous life, until the shadows lengthen and the evening comes, and the fever of life is over and our work is done. Then, of thy great mercy, grant us a safe lodging, and a holy rest, and peace at the last, through Jesus Christ our Lord. Amen.

MRS. PERKINS: Thank you. I know that God has been near in these last days. When I was at the hospital with Mr.

Perkins, I prayed often—especially when I was out in the hall—I would bow my head and ask for God's guidance, and suddenly I'd find myself ready to go into the room again and be unafraid.

PASTOR: I've known that you've been strengthened.

Farewells were said. In evaluating the pastor wrote, "I wanted to bring comfort to this woman and to help her in any way in which need was evident. I had had many contacts with her in the past, and this was a contact, I think, of friend with friend after expected tragedy. I felt that our relationship during this call was close. I'm not so sure that I brought comfort. I think that I jumped from one subject to another too quickly. Perhaps I carried the conversation and did not give her sufficient opportunity to say what was in her mind and heart."

It is probably true that the pastor made some mistakes of a technical character in this call. He pressed Mrs. Perkins a bit hard to get her to accept that a miracle had taken place. He resorted to verbal reassurance on at least two occasions when a simple indication of understanding would have been better. And yet, even with the technical errors, I would have judged this call as much more affirmative and successful than he did if it had been mine.

This pastor had studied the recent research on grief, especially that done under the direction of Erich Lindemann at the Massachusetts General Hospital. He had grasped the vital point of that research on acute grief—that there needs to be a facing of the stark sense of loss, and the suffering that goes with it, before the rebuilding of life on new foundations can be started. He knew that this might assume different forms in different people, but that such reactions as apathy, sentimentality, denial of loss, and others should be seen as inability to face the pain of loss.

If Mrs. Perkins had wept during his visit, or paced up and down and said she felt lost, or shown signs of wanting to talk in detail about her last days with her husband, the pastor with his knowledge of acute grief would have felt easier in his mind. Emotion would have been higher; and for him to be able to accept it, understand it, and not make Mrs. Perkins feel guilty because she had it would have convinced him that he was really being useful.

If Mrs. Perkins' situation had been one of acute grief, the pastor would have been right. If Mr. Perkins had died suddenly of a heart attack, or been killed in an accident, all this would have been true. In that case the response which we see Mrs. Perkins giving in this interview would have been inappropriate and close to apathy.

But that is not the situation. Mrs. Perkins' grief, in the psychological sense of enforced adjustment to loss, did not begin with her husband's death. It began at the time of the unsuccessful surgical operation, eight weeks ago. She has been undergoing what Lindemann calls "anticipatory grief." The acute phase of the "grief work," as Freud called it, ended before Mr. Perkins' death.

Whether the pastor did an effective job on helping Mrs.

Perkins with acute grief cannot, therefore, be seen from the reported contact. To evaluate that we would have to go back and see what he did when news came from the surgeon that the cancer was inoperable. What he has done has been to apply the criteria appropriate to that situation to the reported interview, where they do not fit. He is, therefore, unnecessarily restrained in his favorable comments about his work here.

The reported interview can be evaluated only in the light of Mrs. Perkins' present condition and of the pastor's series of previous contacts with her. Her present condition is not one of acute grief, but of consolidating a now realized but long-anticipated bereavement—and in addition readjusting from a daily schedule which had been very demanding and centered exclusively on her husband. The pastor senses the fatigue, but not its origin in the sense of there now being nothing useful to do when before there was so much.

The pastor's previous contacts have been, so far as we can tell, very helpful to Mrs. Perkins. He no doubt felt he was useful at the time of the surgery. But thereafter, when emotion was less high, he interprets his relationship as "friend with friend." By this what he seems to mean is that he was standing by and giving support, but not helping in any dramatic or specific sense. The latter may be true; and there was no doubt real friendliness in him as he did it. But the fact remains that during those eight weeks, when Mrs. Perkins was going through anticipatory grief, the pastor seemed unaware that he was helping her through it as a pastor by standing by—and was not just a personal friend.

This seems to be an instance, therefore, in which the pastor has very nearly the most helpful attitude all along, so far as our data permit us to judge, in which his timing is good—but all "by ear." The kind of thing he did in the recorded contact was also well timed, one of a series of standing by and supporting pastoral interviews—but not understood by him in its proper setting.

But one may ask: If this pastor had good timing, what difference does it make whether he knew it or not? The answer is that it makes a great deal of difference, not only because he might not guess so well in other situations, but also in his dealings with Mrs. Perkins.

With his concentration upon something more dramatic than is evident in this interview he would of course be alert if strong emotion began to emerge. But acute grief has passed, and this is unlikely. Instead, something of a different order is likely to emerge in a few days, for example, a feeling of uselessness in Mrs. Perkins. This may not be strongly expressed and may be associated by her with the need for resting. The pastor may find himself in a position of urging her to rest, but attempting to talk her out of her feeling of uselessness!

If he had not only used good timing but knew why it was good timing, then by this stage he would see that acute grief has passed but that readjustment is still going to require dealing with negative feelings, though in low rather than high pitch. He would then see that a feeling of uselessness is natural and need not become a permanent character trait if treated as the aftermath of strong reactive emotion. He would also not be misled into too much talk about the importance of resting, since he would know that the fatigue does not come chiefly out of the physical efforts which Mrs. Perkins has put forth.

What the young pastor did was to take the knowledge he had of acute and sudden grief situations and in his thinking apply them to other situations in which they did not apply. But his practice was superior to his thinking. He was more aware of real needs than he knew. Up to a point he could do good work without knowing why. But eventually, even in this case, his lack of awareness that he was applying his generalization to the wrong specific instance would handicap him. If he had not done so well by ear, his error would have been much more obvious.

There is timing, but there is also awareness of timing. A great part of pastoral work is undramatic and non-acute. Much of it is not counseling in the narrower sense of that term, but is an aiding of people to move to the point where they seek counseling when and if they need it. There is some danger that, in our very essential concern for counseling, we not put such a premium upon it that we forget it is useful only if its timing is right. And we can evaluate the timing only if we consider why.

Paul Tillich has reminded us how often the word *kairos* is used in the New Testament as implying the fullness of time, the right or ripe time, the appropriate time—instead of merely *chronos,* the extension of time.

In a small way, but one which may nevertheless mean life or death on occasion, there is a *kairos* in pastoral care. The pastor is not a mere blind instrument where the counseling *kairos* is concerned. By understanding what he can of the processes in operation he can be more sensitive to the true *kairos* in the situation. What might otherwise be adjudged dull contacts may light up with new meaning. "To everything there is a season."

EMBARRASSMENT IN COUNSELING

*Y*OUNG MINISTERS ARE OFTEN ALL TOO CON-scious of their embarrassment in situations that are new to them. The first funeral to conduct, the first prayer with a dying man, the first discussion of a divorce that comes to him—all these and others make him aware of his inexperience. He would like nothing better than to find a way out of his embarrassment.

Most ministers of experience feel different. They would not say they are without embarrassment, and might cite a shakiness and humility while going into the pulpit and evaluate this as a good thing in view of the preacher's responsibility to try to preach the Word of God. But after much experience has been garnered in pastoral work, there is rarely the consciousness of embarrassment that has so plagued their first days in the ministry.

It is by no means clear that this decreasing consciousness of embarrassment is always a good thing. It is surely more comfortable to live and work without it. And its absence is an unalloyed blessing if the experience which has dispelled it has been reflective, that is, if one has learned through his experience not only to feel better but to do better. But this implies that the decrease of embarrassment has not been accompanied by a decrease in sensitivity to the true individuality of each situation.

The absence of embarrassment, however, is not necessarily good if sensitivity has declined along with it. There is a kind of learning from experience which merely puts calluses over the tender spots, so that both pain and sensitivity are lost at the same time. In losing embarrassment one may also lose needed sensitivity to the genuine novelty and depth in new situations. Familiar with and unembarrassed by this type of situation, he is no longer sufficiently self-critical to be aware of its individuality.

The question then becomes: How can we learn from our embarrassment so that we lose it without losing our sensitivity to the individual depth in each situation? To suggest what is involved in answering I want to present a pastoral interview in a hospital situation.

A young and very inexperienced minister whom we shall call William Marr was pastor of a small church in a smallish town. The town was progressive enough to have a hospital, in which Mr. Marr called several times a week.

Because of the closeness of small-town life Mr. Marr had met the Kane family on several occasions, although they were not members of his church. They were, however, Protestants. Mrs. Kane, the middle-aged mother of the family, was rather active in community affairs.

Mr. Marr knew that, about a year ago, Mrs. Kane had discovered she had cancer. She had gone to the hospital and had treatments; then returned home and continued her family and community activities. The cancer continued to become worse, and finally some days before the present interview Mrs. Kane had capitulated and gone back to the hospital. Knowing that Mrs. Kane's church was at this time without a minister, Mr. Marr says, "I decided to make a hospital call." This, incidentally, suggests an alertness to human need which makes us think well of him.

As Mr. Marr entered Mrs. Kane's room at the hospital (he does not tell us whether he cleared first with the nurse), he found her lying with her face toward the wall and crying softly with pain. He waited a few seconds, and then the following took place.

MARR: Hello, Mrs. Kane. It's Bill Marr (*no reply; the sobbing continues*). You are feeling pretty bad, aren't you? (*She still makes no reply, but a gesture indicates she recognizes his presence*). Is there something I can do? Can I call your nurse?

MRS. KANE: (*turning her head to look at him*) They don't let cats or dogs die like this. Why do they let human beings suffer so?

MARR: You are having a pretty hard time of it, aren't you?

MRS. KANE: I pray every night that I won't be here the next morning, but I always am. There was a cancer patient in the next room for a month. She died. From the way she screamed I guess I've got a long way to go yet.

MARR: I think that you must suffer more than we can know

(*pauses, no reply; listens, believes Mrs. Kane is thinking*).
You are having a hard time.

Up to this point Mr. Marr has met a difficult situation extraordinarily well. He knows something about pastoral counseling. Mrs. Kane has been expressing very negative feelings, and he seems to realize correctly that the one chance of getting out more positive feelings is for him to accept the negative feelings as facts and demonstrate that he understands how she can have them. He succeeds therefore in reflecting feeling up to this point, which is what such a situation requires. He may feel uneasy at the high emotion and the unfamiliar situation, but up to this point his embarrassment does not get in the way of what he needs to do as a pastor. Let us move on.

MRS. KANE: Why did this have to happen to me? I've always tried to be good. I've never hurt anybody.

MARR: You don't think that God is being mean to you, do you? You do think that God cares?

Here Mr. Marr shows an entirely different kind of attitude from that which he had previously displayed. Had he been consistent with his former attitude, he would have said something like, "You mean that you don't see what you could have done which would *deserve* this kind of suffering?" Instead, it is as if a bell had rung somewhere inside Mr. Marr. The "Why me?" is the sixty-four dollar theological question. We may imagine that Mr. Marr feels something like this inside, "Up until now I thought I could just be kind of anybody and reflect her feelings; but here she appeals to what I'm supposed to be expert in. This is a theological question, and I'm a kind of theologian. She expects me to have an answer to this one. I guess I must have it somewhere, haven't I? But maybe she doesn't mean it quite as it sounded. Perhaps I could get her to withdraw the question, or cut it down to size." Hence his reply.

The exhibition of Mr. Marr's embarrassment has begun. It has become observable to us not directly, but through the start of his attempts to cover it up. And what brings it out is not just the general unfamiliarity with the situation but his suddenly lost faith in his previous approach. This has disappeared because inwardly he now feels he must meet expectations, have an answer—because a religious question has been asked and he is supposed to have religious answers.

From this point on we can see Mr. Marr's embarrassment increasing.

MRS. KANE: Well, I always have. But it hurts so, and it is so hard to bear.

Here Mrs. Kane makes a concession, showing how the change in his attitude has affected her. But she still feels negative.

MARR: I know it must be. You do have help. Mrs. Brown was telling me the other day she had been up to see you. Don't you think your family and friends really care?

If he had stopped with the first sentence, something constructive might have happened. But by this time he is trying so hard to cover up his own embarrassment at not being able to give her the answer which will plainly help that he tells her, in effect, that she should be grateful for the blessings she has. This is a rejection of her expressed feelings.

MRS. KANE: I suppose they do. They have been good. (*At this point a nurse enters to give her a shot; Mr. Marr goes into the hall and then returns.*) I would like to go home. I don't like the nurses here. They are mean to me.

Mrs. Kane now sees that the deeper and more general negative feelings will not be understood and accepted by Mr. Marr. But she still feels this way and begins to express the feelings in smaller areas, first about the way the hospital treats her.

MARR: Don't you think they can care for you better here than your family could?

MRS. KANE: Yes, but I worry about my family. Bobby is such a problem. He wouldn't do what we wanted him to. I suppose he will be all right. The head nurse here doesn't like me. She is so mean to me. She lies and tells the doctor that I cry when I don't mean to.

MARR: Do you think she is really being mean to you in particular?

MRS. KANE: It seems like it. Since my doctor went on a trip they haven't given me enough shots. The new doctor doesn't understand.

MARR: Things will change when your own doctor returns. Will that be long?

This is certainly getting out on a very long limb.

MRS. KANE: Only a few days now. But this nurse is so mean. She wouldn't even get me a Bible. One of the other nurses did, though. There it is; look at it. (*Mr. Marr picks it up and finds it dusty.*) I have marked the Twenty-Third Psalm. It helps me to keep my mind off my troubles. Just to try to see what it means.

Mrs. Kane is using a sure-fire method of appealing for sympathy. A head nurse who won't get a Bible!

MARR: It does help you to read in the Bible of the faith others have had in God.

This shows Mrs. Kane that the pastor's attitude will be understanding when she is expressing something he will judge to be positive. But the fact is she still feels negative.

MRS. KANE: I wish Bobby would come to see me. He hasn't been for three weeks. He should come on Sundays, but he says he has homework to do.
MARR: Do you think it is best for him to come frequently?

Here he rejects her feelings flatly. But standing on the moral rightness of the child's welfare does not help him to help Mrs. Kane.

MRS. KANE: Yes he should. I am his mother. He is just out playing while I am here suffering so.

MARR: Don't you think it is hard for a boy to see his mother suffer so?

MRS. KANE: Maybe so, but I should know that he cares. It is so hard for me.

MARR: Your husband comes frequently?

MRS. KANE: Yes, every night. But I wish he wouldn't always come at night. I am tired at night. I ask him not to stay long. He really doesn't understand. I don't have much to hold on to.

MARR: Your faith in God and in your friends has helped you much this far. You must continue to believe that others do care. May I pray with you?

Since Mrs. Kane continues to express only negative feeling, the minister has concluded that he cannot really help her. By this time his embarrassment is under control, that is, not showing. When she took what seemed to him an unmotherly line about her son, he corrected her. After all, he has no doubt concluded, you can't help people who won't be helped. So his conscious embarrassment is largely gone. And this enables him to take the bull by the horns and give an exhortation about what she *must* do, following it up with a prayer suggestion which is most difficult for anyone to refuse. This puts his exhortation beyond the realm of discussion. The prayer which followed, and which concluded the call, may be mercifully omitted.

The effect of this call on Mr. Marr was considerable. He wrote: "I think I did a poor job. I'm sure that Mrs. Kane was not much helped, and I know that I didn't fully recover from the call for days. It isn't bad to watch people die, but it is hard to see them fight the inevitable so hard. I thought at one time (months ago) Mrs. Kane had a good attitude toward her trouble. Now I consider it to be terrible. I don't know what to do for the woman. There is no solution for her problem. A changed attitude would help her a lot, but I'm not sure how to get it."

Let us trace the stages in this call around the focus of Mr. Marr's embarrassment. At first the embarrassment existed but did not exhibit itself because it was held in check by his knowledge of counseling—specifically that when negative feelings appear the pastor tries to accept and understand them instead of brushing them aside. This is what we may consider a legitimate protection against the showing of feelings of embarrassment which one may have.

But then came the "Why me?" question, and Mr. Marr felt his own embarrassment. To ward it off he first tried to make at least some slight change in Mrs. Kane's negative feelings and her expectations of him. He told her what she ought to be grateful for. As she brought up negative feelings toward nurse, hospital, and son, he became more and more direct in telling her she ought not to feel as she did. From his point of view the one positive feeling she expressed was about the psalm, and he accepted that. But all her other statements were negative, and he met them, one might say, with increasing assurance in his disagreement. This meant that his consciousness of his embarrassment dwindled as the call continued.

This does not mean the embarrassment itself diminished. Indeed, it may have increased. Not only was Mr. Marr affected for days by the call; but he became so desperately embarrassed that he said things at the end which, having written them up, he was quite sure were very wrong, and which he would not have considered saying under other circumstances.

Embarrassment was threat. Increasingly strong measures were used to control it, to put the awareness of it out of existence. But the embarrassment, repressed, continued. Indeed, it was so strong that even in writing up the call the pastor was unable to learn very much from his experience. The threat was still so much with him, and so personal, that he could express only a generalized feeling of failure and uneasiness.

Yet he could have learned—and later, I think, did learn —much from study of himself in this experience. He could see that his initial embarrassment in entering on a new and highly charged situation need not be a handicap —and that the embarrassment which caused him difficulty, and made necessary his unhelpful measures of defense, grew out of a false notion of his function in such situations. Had he been able to retain his initial embarrassment inside, the minor tension which this caused in him would not have impeded his pastoral work. In a later similar situation this normal embarrassment would have been a bit less, owing to his experience. After much experience he would be unembarrassed in the first sense and still retain his sensitivity.

As it is, and unless he learns from this call, his problem will not be with the initial and natural embarrassment at all. What he will do will be to concentrate on not feeling embarrassed, that is, making himself feel confident in situations of this kind. He may develop some kind of routine for all such calls. Or he may become hearty, or begin his exposition of the silver linings immediately on entering the room. Whatever he does of this kind will be a defensive device against recognizing his own embarrassment—the secondary embarrassment arising out of a wrong notion of his function, not the primary embarrassment arising out of finding himself in an unfamiliar situation.

The general point seems to be that our first embarrassment on entering an unfamiliar situation is natural, understandable, and need not impede our ability to help in any significant degree. If we recognize it as such and inwardly accept it, we do then learn from our later experience; and we eventually lose this kind of embarrassment without losing our sensitivity to individuality.

But where secondary embarrassment enters, hitting us so strongly that we automatically resort to measures of defense, then harm may come both immediately and in the long run. We may succeed in *feeling* unembarrassed, but at the cost of a real loss in sensitivity. Direct efforts to relieve or allay this kind of embarrassment will betray rather than help us.

Secondary embarrassment is a form of anxiety. In situations like that of Mr. Marr with Mrs. Kane it rests upon a false feeling about the nature of one's helping function. Why did Mr. Marr feel threatened at perhaps not having the answer to a religious problem raised by Mrs. Kane? Both theologically and psychologically we know that no person can ever completely and surely give the exact religious interpretation which will be assimilable by another. We can give our own answers, and we can give general answers which lead toward the specific; but we cannot give *the* answer for this person, any person. To rest in the illusion that we can is an uncomfortable form of playing God.

We need not know the specific conditions in Mr. Marr's life to enable us to realize that his interest in religion and the ministry—which may be sound at root—nevertheless contains unhealthy elements. If he does not examine those through some such means as what he exhibited in dealing with Mrs. Kane, he will be less helpful to other people, and to his own fulfillment, than if he did so.

Young pastors like Mr. Marr can take justified reassurance from this story about the inevitable embarrassment they will feel in new and strange pastoral work situations. They can learn from their embarrassment if they reflect upon it and put it in its place. If they can separate it from the secondary embarrassment in their reflections, they can learn still more. Eventually their primary embarrassment disappears without loss of sensitivity.

Those of us who are older may also be reassured, though in a different way. Perhaps we may, instead of priding ourselves that youthful embarrassment has gone, be more alert to its presence when we are in certain types of situations. We may thereby be coming closer to our own emotional centers of gravity and may the better insure that our absence of embarrassment has not been achieved at the cost of depth in communicating with those we would serve.

Chapter Nine

*O*UT OF A SENSE OF PROFESSIONAL DUTY I once read a course issued by one of the numerous "charm schools." It proved more illuminating than I had supposed. Intended for women (the male equivalent is a "success school"), it had mostly common sense remarks to make about keeping the hair, nails, hips, bust, body hair, warts, and stenographer's spread well in hand—so *he* would notice. The main thrust was much closer to the original meaning of charm as allurement or enticement than the vendors may have suspected.

But there were occasional notes of a different kind, suggestions that if the would-be charmer wanted to get somewhere she would have to *be* what she wanted to look like. Where the hairdo and hip-culture were not too bizarre, this notion seemed to have merit. It is true that the chief end of charm still seemed to be to rope them in, but even a hint that rope would not permanently hold them was a kind of concession to spiritual veracity.

I have been thinking recently of charm in counseling, and whether there may be an underground note of truth in the compulsion to be enticing which can so easily wreck a counseling opportunity. Can we assess the meaning of such a tendency so as to transform it for good?

A major form in which the charm compulsion appears in ministers is the good-fellow complex. We clergy are supposed to have, and often do have, an occupational hazard in the form of social pressure to play at being the professional good men of the community. Falling into the pressure, we may become pompous in bearing, sepulchral in intonation, tuned up to give the proper degree of shock on contact with the common or vulgar or profane in life. Most of us resist this and want to be good fellows instead—not "Sweet Adeline" at two o'clock in the morning, but clearly human beings and not exhibitions of stiffness and unctuousness. So we may work a bit hard at being good fellows—sliding into third at the Sunday-school picnic, playing golf occasionally with the chairman of deacons, discussing a movie as a sermon illustration, and performing a spot of baby-kissing now and then. This is charm.

In itself charm may be what Luther called "adiaphora"—the neutral things that do not need to matter one way or the other. It may also perform a positive function. For the minister who fails to show that he is like other people is usually assumed, rightly or wrongly, to be of a different order, and may never get close to his people. If charm is exercised under compulsion, however, it will likely be harmful regardless of whether or not the form it takes shows good taste or not.

Fred, a young theological student, was a leader at a summer camp. In the group which he was shepherding was Irene, whose family Fred had known in another connection although he had not previously known Irene. Irene was sixteen, but large and mature-looking for her age, friendly in manner without being aggressive. She had impressed Fred as being "competent, genuine, and wholesome." Near the end of the week's conference she asked Fred if she might talk with him. Time and place were set for the same day.

FRED: Well, tell me, Irene, how goes it? How have you liked your first conference?

IRENE: I've liked it a lot. It's really fun. The kids are all so friendly.

FRED: Has it been what you expected?

IRENE: Yes—I think so—but that's what I want to ask you about.

FRED: Yes?

IRENE: The thing that bothers me is about when I get home.

FRED: You mean this has been such a wonderful experience that you don't know how to make it last?

IRENE: Well, sort of. You see, I live in a very small town, where there isn't much to do or anything. Our church is real small too—and, well, I just don't see why the kids aren't interested—but they're not, and I don't know what to do about it!

FRED: You mean you think they ought to take a more active part in things?

IRENE: Yes, all they seem to care about is dates and dances and stuff.

FRED: And you wish they'd be interested in the church instead?

IRENE: Well, you see, we have an old minister—really old enough to retire—and of course the kids don't like him too well. They think he's old-fogeyish.

FRED: Tell me, aren't you interested in dates too?

Up to this point Fred has done a pretty good job of helping Irene get started on whatever she wants to say. But at this point his desire to be charming, to show he's a good fellow who doesn't disapprove of "dates and dances and stuff," has got the better of him as a counselor.

IRENE: No, not particularly.

FRED: (*kiddingly*) Why, Irene, we'll have to find out about this! It's part of life, you know!

IRENE: Yes, I suppose so—but, well, the boys in town are so silly.

FRED: (*laughing*) Yes, I know what you mean. When I was your age, I thought so too—about girls! Of course it takes boys a little longer to grow up than it does girls.

IRENE: Yes, I know. I have three brothers.

FRED: All older?

IRENE: Yes.

FRED: Then you must be the baby of the family?

IRENE: (*a little vehemently*) I *am*.

FRED: You mean you wish you weren't?

IRENE: Well, I think it's hard for my parents to remember what it's like to be my age.

FRED: Why, I should have thought that Esther and your brothers would have paved the way for you!

IRENE: Yeah, I guess they did—in a way. But that's another thing. My father just won't go to church.

FRED: You mean he's not interested—or he's "agin" it?

We may note the charm compulsion in the slang "agin."

IRENE: Oh, he's changed so. He treats Mother just awful. And he didn't used to be that way.

FRED: What happened to change him? Do you know?

IRENE: Well, when I was little we lived in Middletown. Father was a teacher in the high school there. The school board wanted him to play politics, and he wouldn't so they made it tough for him in town, and the next year he resigned. Of course several members of the school board were church members; so Daddy thinks now that everybody in the church is a hypocrite.

FRED: Before this happened, was he interested in the church?

IRENE: Yes, both he and Mother were.

FRED: And what about your mother now?

IRENE: Oh, she still goes—but Daddy makes her life miserable every time she does. Oh, he's *so* mean to her (*becoming more emotional*).

FRED: Well, now just what do you mean by that? You mean he makes it hard for her by what he says, or what?

IRENE: Oh, you have no idea—what awful things he says to her. And he's so inconsiderate—sometimes I think he does things *just* to make it hard for her. And nothing she ever does is right. But she just takes it and says nothing.

FRED: Of course she probably understands what it is that has made him bitter—and that he's sort of taking it out on her—don't you think?

Here it becomes clear that the charm compulsion extends rather widely over Fred's life, for at this point he wants to show how smart he is. He is not only not concentrating on Irene's feelings but is falling into her distortions; he does not seem to see the mother's reaction as of the doormat variety.

IRENE: I suppose so. But I do wish he'd go to church. I've tried every way I know to do something about it, but he just won't listen to either Mother or me.

FRED: You think going to church would help him?

IRENE: Oh, I don't know. He doesn't like our minister either, thinks he's a hypocrite too.

FRED: Then maybe going to church wouldn't be of much help to him?

This whole point is irrelevant, was brought in by Fred. If it did not work one way, he would try the other. The one thing accomplished is to show his charm. But at the same time Irene is diverted from saying what she really feels.

IRENE: (*smiling*) Well, maybe not. But it would sure make it easier for Mother

FRED: Does he make it hard for both you and your mother when you go to church?

IRENE: He does for Mother, but he just thinks I'm silly to bother.

FRED: Then he must not be very sympathetic with your sister's school plans?

IRENE: No, he won't help her at all.

FRED: Well, tell me, what have you done about all this, your father, the kids, and so on?

IRENE: I haven't known what to do—but I've prayed about it. Of course now I'm not even sure there is a God! Is it awful to think that?

FRED: Why? Why should it be? Not at all. Sometimes by

doubting things we've always been taught we begin to learn things for ourselves. But why do you think there maybe isn't any God?

Fred's idea is good, but the motive for handling it this way is charm.

IRENE: Well, I've never really felt him very near. How does one really *know* there is a God anyway?

FRED: Well, if by knowing you mean that you want to touch or feel him, the answer is that you can't. But there are such things in the world as love, hate, fear—feelings like those your father has which you certainly can't see or touch or feel with your fingers, but you know they are there; don't you? (*Irene smiles with comprehension.*) It's sort of the same way with God. Then too there are so many things in our universe that are orderly—the sun always rises in the east, day always follows night, spring, winter, and so on. And somehow you just can't tell me that it all just happened. But most important of all, when one has once sensed his guidance and his presence, there just never is any doubt again. See?

I don't, and I don't believe Irene did either; but then she is more polite than I.

IRENE: But you don't think it's awful for me to doubt?

FRED: Not at all—as I said, only in that way will you work out a faith that is *yours,* and not secondhand. Just keep at it, in the thinking process. (*Dinner bell rings, and Irene makes no move.*) Well, what say you? Do you need to get ready for dinner?

IRENE: Yes, I guess so. But thanks so very much for letting me talk with you.

What did Fred himself think of it? He wrote: "Almost from the beginning it was obvious that Irene had come to talk over something more serious than just the kids at church. However, it was somewhat difficult to know whether it was the situation in regard to boys and dates, her home situation, her religious doubts, or all of them combined. In the course of the interview we touched on all of them, but may not have probed deeply enough into any one to be of real help to her. In fact it seemed almost as though when we got near the vital part of each one either she or I changed the course of the conversation. Throughout I missed several points and redirected the course of the thinking—unfortunately. Also I failed to respond always to Irene's feelings, doing it only sporadically. In several instances I rejected irrelevant comments and personal references which did not help. While I am certain that Irene did not get the maximum of help, I do think she was benefited to some degree by talking her problems over with someone whom she trusted and respected."

Fred knows something about counseling. He realized how often he got sidetracked from concentrating on Irene's feelings. He is puzzled because Irene did not stick to some one problem area, but at least he senses that various problem areas may all be tied up together. But what is clear to us is that he overlooks entirely the function which his need to be charming performed in the contact. Although he concludes his evaluation with a modest statement that Irene was helped a bit because she "trusted and respected" him, he does not see that getting what he calls trust and respect was the *sine qua non* of the whole situation for him—that without which he would feel an utter failure. In straining so hard to get it, he gave no help to Irene and may even have confused her further by telling her how understanding he was and yet not demonstrating real understanding at all.

It looks very much, therefore, as if Fred's compulsion to be charming—like Karen Horney's "neurotic need for affection"—is entirely concealed from him. It seems to be a strategy which he *must* use automatically without awareness that he is doing so. It seems, in other words, to be a neurotic trend or pattern, with no insight in Fred about it.

When Fred submitted this contact report to me as his instructor, I wrote him a direct comment on it—not as direct and personal as what has been said above, but fairly direct nevertheless. I put it in the form of a question: Since it seemed clear that Irene did not get much clarification by the end of the contact, could it be that the deviations from what Fred knew about how to proceed in counseling came out of a kind of inability to refrain from making an impression in a particular fashion? I reasoned that this was put indirectly enough so that Fred would not have to accept it if unprepared to do so, but directly enough so that it might give him a boost to examine it if he were ready.

It turned out that he was quite ready to do so—at least so long as the discussion we had resolved around his professional function. During the contact itself he had had suspicions that there was a reason why he was doing what he knew would not help. When he wrote it up, his suspicions grew. Apparently the word that helped him get his finger on it was "strategy." As soon as it occurred to him that there might really be an explorable reason why he deviated from what he knew should be done in counseling, that very thought released him in a measure from the compulsion. This was not direct personal therapy for Fred. The compulsion may reach deeply into his life, and he might need psychotherapy over a period of time to get it thoroughly in hand. But he could make some progress on it in his professional activities in any case, and that was the intention of my efforts. We discussed this distinction to make sure he would understand it.

But if Fred could so quickly get some light on the self-defeating character of his charm compulsion, at least in his counseling, then two conclusions follow. First, this was not so deep-seated as to be entirely inaccessible to conscious reflection. Second, it was not without a kind of positive as well as negative meaning.

Most obviously it had negative meaning. He will not gain by nursing it. For if he does, he will go on diverting people he is trying to help. But the *intention* of the need to be charming is partially positive. It implies a desire to be related to other people in a way which will help them.

117

If this is freed from compulsive elements, then it can be a virtue. Fred may have some distance to go. But he has made genuine progress even in analyzing this one contact.

Let us suppose that Fred, without a compulsion to be charming, had followed what we would regard as the best counseling approach and method in his contact with Irene. Irene would then have concentrated more firmly on examining her own feelings and problems, and would have gained more clarification. At the end of the contact she might not have said verbally how much she had gained from this, for she would be working it over in such a way that she would not have to think of the amenities. But a bit later she might think back upon it and be grateful to Fred in a thoroughly rational way for helping her to see some of the insights. If what Fred wants is to be genuinely helpful, this would give it to him vastly better than what he actually did. It would not of course be so immediate or obvious, but it would be much more real. His intention therefore can better be fulfilled without the compulsion. For the function of the compulsion is to get it now, get the *signs* of it now—and hence one gets the shadow without the substance. Freed from that, one may get the real thing.

If we find in our counseling an element of the charm compulsion, it will do little good to call it bad names and try to legislate it out. We do well to recognize how effective it can be in destroying counseling opportunities.

But if we also realize that the intention behind it contains much that is positive, we may find that we can begin to destroy the compulsive element in our counseling and free the genuine desire to help people so that it succeeds in doing so.

HOSTILITY IN COUNSELING

Chapter Ten

*A*PERENNIAL PROBLEM IN PASTORAL COUN-
seling is how to deal with a parishioner who has sought
counseling and yet becomes hostile or aggressive during
the process. The usual answer is that, if such hostility
arises, we should "accept" it, not fight it, be understanding
of it, and perhaps then help the person to look at it himself. If it persists, the implication is that we are being
coercive and are therefore feeding it.

For gross situations this is a good explanation and a
good prescription. But it is sometimes rather thin for the
pastor who has had training in counseling, who knows
how to follow a parishioner's leads, and who has had
enough successful experiences with people to make him
sure he does not arouse aggressiveness in the ordinary
sense.

A pastoral counseling experience which seems to shed
significant light on this problem recently came to me from
a minister in his thirties, who has excellent knowledge
and skill in counseling. With his permission I present the
story with his analysis and my analysis of his analysis,

in order to attempt to clarify ways of dealing with hostility in counseling.

Betty, the heroine or villain of the story, was in her late teens at the time of the pastoral interviews which follow. She was attractive, active in numerous church affairs, and a member of the choir in the church. A year before, she had finished high school and taken a job in another town. She did not do well in the work, was released from her job, and returned home disgruntled. When the minister had seen her casually, she had appeared unpredictable and temperamental. She vacillated between cordial friendliness and critical hostility. She had stuck barbs into the pastor on two or three occasions in casual meetings.

Betty was the older daughter in a family which seemed in general to be on the defensive, critical and bitter. Her father was an excellent craftsman, but instead of holding regular jobs or hunting them up he spent most of his time puttering around his own home. This created a financial problem at home, and Betty's mother spent a good deal of her time doing housework in the community in order to keep them going.

After a Sunday evening service Betty approached the pastor. She seemed to him more subdued than usual and asked if he would talk with her later that evening. An appointment was made, and Betty returned at the appointed time.

BETTY: I'm surprised you even talk to me, the way I've acted toward you.

MINISTER: Well, I've tried to understand that your actions were not directed toward me personally so much as just lashing out with some of the mixed-up forces inside of you.

BETTY: I've felt mixed up for a long time. There seemed to be strange forces going on inside of me, but I didn't know what they were. I just knew that I was unhappy. At first I didn't understand what you were preaching about, but then I gradually realized that you were describing some of the things going on inside of me, and I began to see what they were.

MINISTER: Sort of like shining a flashlight down on the swirling waters of a river in the darkness and seeing some of the currents.

BETTY: Sort of, yes, and now that I see it I'm scared. I'm afraid of what's going to happen.

MINISTER: It's pretty terrifying to see fantastic forces at work inside one.

BETTY: I'm afraid even you would be shocked to know what's going on inside me.

MINISTER: I think I've heard or experienced about everything. You couldn't shock me.

BETTY: I caught myself recently daydreaming of Jean, and I realized that what I was doing was thinking of how I could kill her—not that I would, but there must be something terribly wrong with me to think such thoughts. I'm afraid I'm on the road to becoming crazy.

MINISTER: You must resent Jean very much.

BETTY: (*with deep intensity*) I hate her. (*after a moment*) Oh, I don't really hate her—she is my sister. But I hate her ways. She is getting more spoiled and insolent every day. You can't tell her anything. She gets her own way all the time—Dad makes a baby out of her. She knows she can get anything she wants from him. She's so smug about it I can't stand her.

MINISTER: How does your father treat the rest of you?

BETTY: He cares nothing about us at all. All he can do is criticize. Nothing satisfies him.

MINISTER: Part of your resentment against Jean, then, is your resentment that your father doesn't think as much of you as he does of her. Is that right?

BETTY: I suppose that is partly it. But I've talked with Mother, and I know how miserable life has been with him. The way he's treated her, I have no faith in men. I hate men.

MINISTER: All men are basically like your father?

BETTY: I've known a lot of them, and they're all the same. I went out with them for a good time, but at heart I detested all of them, and I told them so, too.

Since this was written up by the minister from memory, it is a summary and not the entire conversation, which took about twice as long as the above words would suggest. At the concluding point the pastor asked if Betty would like to go on with this the following day, and Betty said she would. When she arrived at the appointed time next day, the pastor sensed a bit of constraint in her from the beginning. Her ambivalent attitude was back.

BETTY: It seems silly for me to be coming down here to talk with you.

MINISTER: You don't think I can help you, is that it?

BETTY: The whole thing makes you out to be so superior. That's what I always detested about you. You always seemed so sure of yourself. You'd never strike back when I'd say something nasty to you. You always act as though you are so superior.

MINISTER: Yes, I suppose you might get that impression of me. My defense against your attacks was to ignore them and be just the same toward you as the others.

BETTY: But you seemed so self-confident that I resented it.

MINISTER: Anybody who has strength in himself is sort of a threat to you?

BETTY: You made me feel even more inferior.

MINISTER: Coming to me now makes you feel the same way?

BETTY: You're thinking to yourself how superior you are. You think you're helping me, but inside I'm laughing at you.

MINISTER: On the one hand you feel you need help, that something is wrong with you; but on the other hand you resent being helped. Even if I could help you, you would defeat me in order to show that you are really superior to me?

BETTY: That's right. I'll not give you the satisfaction of thinking you're better than I am. There's really not much use to this, because all the time I'm laughing at you and thinking how stupid you are not to realize it.

MINISTER: (*this* "*stung.*") It seems from what you have told me that you are the one who is being stupid. You are laughing at me, but you are actually defeating yourself, not me. You have a problem which is bothering you, but you are, as it were, cutting off your nose to spite your own face. It really doesn't affect me. You are the one who will continue to suffer.

From this point on, the pastor reports, the case was lost. Betty switched her attack to another girl in the youth group of whom she knew the pastor thought highly. She moved on to criticize the whole church, then the community. By this time the pastor was so thoroughly on the defensive that he attempted explicitly to point out to her that, even if her criticisms were correct, her feelings betrayed hostility which was a projection of her feeling of being rejected. Betty could accept none of this and came back with more recriminations. The interview wore itself out in something like bickering, and any possibility of counseling was destroyed.

Casual relationships were maintained by the pastor with Betty for several years. Through a number of unhappy life experiences Betty gained a little insight into the fact that some of her difficulties were due to her own attitude. She fell very much in love once and idealized the young man; but when this broke up, she realized that her own attitude, including the idealization, had had something to do with his leaving.

Her new insights went only a certain distance, however. Finally she left home and the home town altogether and went to a large city. The pastor had one brief contact with her there. She boasted that she was living "fast and loose," and liked it. Her attitude seemed to be a kind of flaunting herself at society. She boasted of gold digging with men friends and feeling wonderful that she could get expensive clothes and be taken to expensive night clubs.

It is clear that the pastor was far from ignorant of how to go about effective counseling. His first few comments, for example, show an excellent ability to follow leads, that is, to grasp the essential thing Betty is trying to convey, show her in his own words that he understands it, and thus contribute to clarification of what she means.

Nor is he coercive or aggressive in any ordinary sense,

at least until the last part of the second contact in which he tries desperate measures because he believes he has already failed in counseling. There is no "Now look here, young woman," in his voice. Nor does he imply, "If you will see this from my point of view, it will be all right." Obvious coercion is absent.

And yet he failed. The failure stuck in his mind sufficiently for him to write up the interviews and later analyze them because he believed he had a crucial opportunity with Betty and muffed it. He asked himself whether it was he who failed, or whether anyone would have failed with Betty at that time in spite of her apparent desire for help.

As he reflected later upon the situation, here is what he wrote: "Although I was aware of the dynamic factors in Betty's make-up, I nevertheless responded much of the time to the idea content of what she was saying rather than to her feelings. I was intent upon getting her to understand the forces at work within her, so intent that I did not pause sufficiently to understand how she saw it and felt about it. I told her I understood, but I threw away my best chances to demonstrate that, for example, when I said, 'How does your father treat the rest of you?'

"I did convey some understanding. The interviews, especially the first, did in a measure give her opportunity to see something of the compulsive attitude she had toward other people. This might eventually have been the entree to some of the factors underlying her hostility and self-rejection, but she was not yet ready to see these things. I suppose the answer is that I was too emotionally insecure myself to let her proceed at her own pace. My very anxiety to get her to see what was going on inside her accentuated her hostility. And behind the hostility was distrust of herself.

"I understood the two-sidedness of her attitude and was even able to state it. But when I came up against it, and she directed it toward me, instead of discussing it in general, I was more concerned to bolster myself by proving I was a capable counselor than I was to follow through the implications of my knowledge.

"I clearly failed after the point where I said, 'You don't think I can help you, is that it?' As I see it now, I was myself confused. I recognized the irrational quality in the hostility she was directing at me; and yet I knew there was some validity in the insight she had into my attitude, for I was nursing a secret notion that a counselor was thereby superior to people he helped.

"When she turned her hostility on me, therefore, I was vulnerable, for I reacted in such a way that she should not be able to show her superiority. My response was full of my own resentment, therefore, even more so than the words on paper suggest. At the time I thought I was merely being firm, intent on not being worked, putting cards on the table, in order to retain her respect. Actually, I was merely reacting. She sensed this, and therefore attacked me, though indirectly. I was then reduced to argument.

"Had I been able to accept her hostility toward me and

been big enough to understand it, I believe this might have got her started toward clarification of her feelings. But there is a big *if* there, really meaning that I would have had to be a different person in the situation.

"As I see it now, Betty was so hostile that she was prepared to interpret almost anything from the outside in a hostile way. I did not see this at the time. Consequently, although what I said seemed to be understanding, it was in fact not so."

So far as it goes, and it goes a long distance, this pastor's analysis of his failure seems correct. He was not coercive or aggressive in the usual sense of those words. But from the point where he said, "You couldn't shock me," he was secretly on the defensive. At that place in the first contact, he began to concentrate on the impression he was making on Betty, that is, his own superiority as a counselor, rather than on understanding and accepting Betty herself. At the point where he said, "You couldn't shock me," he might have said instead: "You mean it seems pretty terrible?"

This concentration on his own place in the situation continues when the minister says, "You must resent Jean very much." Something like, "This idea is really disturbing you," would have communicated understanding much better. The pastor himself points out the mistake at the point where he said, "How does your father treat the rest of you?" Here, and also where he says, "All men are basically like your father?" the pastor is following the literal counseling book, but in a subtle way he is forcing

Betty to admit there is something wrong with her attitude —instead of understanding what the attitude is with which Betty is already dissatisfied.

The defensiveness becomes more marked in the second contact. What the pastor says at the beginning, "You don't think I can help you, is that it?" puts Betty's back up, and it remains arched through the contract. What he should have done instead was to accept the divided feelings Betty had about coming, especially the hostility. He might have said, "Well, in that case, maybe we ought to look at the silliness first," if he could say it with a friendly grin.

In his analysis of the work the pastor says it was his unconscious idea of himself as a model counselor which betrayed him. He had done some genuinely effective counseling with other people before these contacts with Betty. He did know something about it, and he was not building on illusions. But the fact was he had never before tried to help someone with hostility like Betty's. Therefore, her words became a challenge to him to prove he could be a good counselor; and when she would not accept what he said as he thought he meant it, he could not accept her refusal. So he reacted to hostility with hostility.

The pastor, quite correctly, suggests that he would have had to be a different person to have handled this contact more happily. But he is that different person now; otherwise he could not have seen this so clearly. His very analysis of the situation has pushed ahead his insights not only into counseling but also into himself. And the new insight will be a permanent possession both to him and to his counseling.

Provided our understanding goes deep enough, there is nothing basically more difficult about counseling with hostile people—if they also want help—than with others. We may not get results so often, because the very nature of the hostility-generating personality may be harder to get at. But we can as easily provide a channel for insights to emerge if they are ready to emerge. That is, we can provided our own status is not involved in success or failure with any particular person. If, like the pastor in this situation, we can accept many kinds of attitudes as parts of the problem but cannot accept those which are hostile, the answer is probably to be found in asking ourselves why a hostile attitude in a parishioner who wants help does threaten us. It will be found either there or in our failure to communicate understanding and acceptance of the hostility to the parishioner in spite of our actual acceptance and understanding of it. Generally speaking, the latter is present if the former exists.

Our original question was how we may deal with a parishioner who wants counseling but who nevertheless shows hostility to us as we try to help him. We have seen that, in however subtle a way, the difficulty lies usually not in the hostility itself but in our secret resentment of it, and therefore in our own attitude. The real answer, therefore, is to be found in a further look at ourselves and in the reaction we are making upon the parishioner, even though the reaction be unintentional.

But there is another important point. The pastor did have to go a step further in understanding himself, but he had to do so *operationally,* that is, he had to do so in such a way that he could examine the way this really operated in his counseling work. No doubt it would have been of value if he could have achieved this insight in psychotherapy or counseling in which he was client or patient. But he would still have had to translate its meaning into the professional situation in which he was counselor. In this story the shock of failure in counseling led the pastor to the personal insight by way of the professional situation. He had to see the implications for the counseling he carried out.

In real life he was no autocrat and was a friendly person. In personal relationships his friends would have found it difficult to become angry with him. But when he stepped into his professional role, he assumed unconsciously that he had to defend something. An attack on his skill, and even on his intentions, in counseling was, so to speak, an attack on his gospel. He had not seen this point until Betty unwittingly forced it on him. His professional citadel had been attacked, he thought. But when he understood the whole situation more clearly, he saw that this was not so.

If the pastor had genuinely understood Betty's hostility, and accepted it in the same sense that he felt it understandable that she should have it, would he have succeeded in changing her subsequent life course? We cannot know. It is possible that he might have. But the result would have depended also on Betty's degree of readiness for help, which remains uncertain from the fragments we have.

But suppose no better results had been achieved with Betty, which is possible. It would then have been clear to the pastor that he had done the most that any outsider could have done at this time, that the character-twisting forces had gone so deeply in Betty already that the counseling forces could not help. Even then, however, the situation would have been better. For Betty, understanding more clearly the absence of hostility and resentment in the pastor, would have felt more positively drawn to such a source of help in the future than she actually was. So, win or lose, he would have been helping Betty more.

The general answer to dealing with hostility in counseling, therefore, seems to be looking at ourselves—but looking at ourselves in the counseling context and not just as persons in friendly relationship situations. This should not be implied as a counsel of perfection. Probably no one of us is without some irrational feelings, including hostility and resentment. But an understanding that these exist can itself do much to enable us to eliminate their influence from our counseling.

There are many more subtleties to hostility in counseling than this chapter has discussed. But the central point is believed to be a kind of prerequisite to further discussion: insight into our resentment of hostile reactions, in a counseling context.

CONVICTIONS IN COUNSELING

*W*HAT DOES A PASTOR DO WITH HIS CONVICtions while he is counseling? Does he park his theological, ethical, and social beliefs at the door of the cubicle? Does he try to convert the parishioner to his own views? Or is there some alternative?

If counseling is to be what I have called an "eductive" or leading-out process, invoking strengths and resources which can emerge only through the parishioner, then any attempt to concentrate attention in counseling upon the views of the pastor is wrong because it distracts from placing exclusive attention upon the parishioner. It is plainly wrong if done exploitatively or coercively, because such action would ignore the inherent dignity of the person. But even if the views are right, and the attempt to convert is done without protest from the parishioner, it is still poor counseling because it diverts from what requires concentration in counseling.

But it would be no more satisfactory to assert that the pastor should check his convictions before counseling. To begin with, it cannot be done. If it is a conviction, it

133

goes deep and is not a mere opinion about something one considers indifferent anyhow. The illusion that one had temporarily discarded his convictions would, therefore, merely permit them to operate *sub rosa* in ways of which he would be unaware. Besides, this would return the pastor to the multiple-role theory of the ministry, according to which he would be one personality while preaching, another while educating, and a third while counseling. If the practice of the ministry is to have any unity and integrity—and it has—the pastor must bring the same basic attitude to all facets of his activity, however much the details may be proliferated differently with different functions.

Neither of these answers can be satisfactory. If the pastor has convictions about race relations, world peace, the rights of workers, the value of the church, or the meaning of God, he can neither discard them nor focus attention on them while he counsels.

What *can* he do? To get a positive answer we need to back up for a moment to look at the minister in his total functioning. It is certainly no mystery to his people that the pastor believes in God, is opposed to divorce when marriages can be rehabilitated, believes in eliminating racial segregation, and the like. For in sermons and other ways his personal views have been made known. When any parishioner comes to him for counsel, therefore, it is on the basis of—or in spite of—knowing at least something about these views. Even if the pastor has come but recently to his church, and little is known of his distinctively personal convictions, his people will assume—not always correctly, to be sure—that the very fact of his being a minister implies his belief in some things and not in others.

Since the people know, or think they know, what the pastor's convictions are, they will therefore play a part in counseling whether the minister is aware of it or not. But this implies that the question is not one of *exposition* of the pastor's views but, so far as the pastor's views enter as his views, of *correction*. Let me illustrate. Suppose that Mrs. Brown comes to the pastor to discuss divorcing her husband and says that she knows the pastor is against divorce but she doesn't know whom else to talk with. The pastor may say, "I'm certainly glad to talk with you about this. As a matter of fact, although I believe separation and divorce are desperate remedies, I am not necessarily against either one if holding the family together does no good to its members. But suppose we look at the situation as you see it." If she does not want to go on with the situation defined in those terms and says, "Just what conditions do you believe justify divorce?" the pastor can define more sharply, as by saying, "Well, I suppose I could give a general sermon on the subject. But I take it what we want to get at is the Browns. Why don't we look at your situation, and then perhaps we can see more clearly what is right and wrong in general." There is no reason why the pastor needs to feel himself forced to give an exposition of his own views in this fashion. If Mrs. Brown continues to insist, the pastor may decide that he should expound his views and do so; but in that case he should make it quite clear that this is not counseling, but an extension of his public speaking ministry. He should also tell himself that Mrs. Brown is not ready for counseling with him. If the situation is so defined, people rarely do this.

The chances are very strong that the correction of Mrs. Brown's view of his view is all that is needed and becomes a part of redefining the counseling situation. It can be done quickly and as a help to the counseling process. This is on the ground that the more clearly the nature of the counseling process is understood by both people, the more honest and ultimately helpful it is likely to be. If Mrs. Brown proceeds on the false assumption, throughout the contact, that the pastor is opposed to separation or divorce regardless of circumstances, the situation is unfree and impeded. If a single redefinition, without details, is used to correct her wrong impression, the counseling situation is opened, broadened in its possibilities, and made more free for honest consideration of the issues.

Part of our positive answer to the place of convictions in counseling is, then, that they not only may but should appear briefly as corrective redefinitions when a parishioner attributes to us a view which we do not hold; but that if a regular exposition of our views seems to be necessary, either to us or to him, the situation has at least temporarily ceased to be a counseling relationship.

There is, however, a second aspect to our positive answer. If a parishioner has sought our help at all, and has a conflict or problem, the chances are strong that— if he gets real aid in clarifying—his inner predilections are in the direction of what we stand for, always providing our own convictions make some sense in their own right. Let us revert to Mrs. Brown. If she had no conflict and were quite clear about wanting a divorce, she would go to a lawyer, not a minister. If she wanted a divorce without question, but also desired some counseling which would clarify her inner churnings, it is not very likely that she would seek out a minister, unless he had attained a personal reputation for dealing with such questions on their own merits. She would more probably select someone who could not be suspected of any conviction against divorce.

If she has in fact come to the pastor, that tells something in itself. If she achieves some clarification about her situation, she may see some new ways whereby the marriage can be put on a sounder basis. But we may note that this may not save the marriage, even if Mrs. Brown's predilections are for doing so. Mr. Brown may be a veritable skunk, who will get no help for himself nor change one whit. In that case whether or not Mrs. Brown would go against the pastor's convictions would depend on the nature of those convictions. If his view is legalistic, and what he really wants is to hold the marriage together even at the price of turning Mrs. Brown into a driveling masochist, I would hope he might reconsider the convictions. If his views are what I would regard as deeper and more person-centered, then even separation or divorce might not be against his views, if the evils thereof were likely to be less than the evils of holding the pieces together.

A pastoral contact reported to me by a young pastor we may call Thomas Temple is instructive about the place of convictions in counseling. The contact is with a middle-aged bachelor named Bruce Webster, who is somewhat simple-minded though not moronic. He is a descendant of early settlers of the community and has therefore inherited the highest social status in his town. He has not had much education, however, as contrasted with the rest of the local upper crust.

The town in which the pastor's small church is located is fairly old as American towns go and has had only occasional new settlers within it over the past half century except for a group of Negroes who live in a segregated section. Nearly all the Negroes went there to do straight labor on a railroad and therefore do not have the variety of social classes that would be true in a larger segregated Negro settlement. The rest of the community resents the presence of the Negroes, but most people hasten to add that this is not because they are Negroes but because of their low social and moral standards, drinking, and gambling.

Mr. Webster is an active member of Mr. Temple's church. One Sunday afternoon, as Temple was coming out of the church, Webster stopped him:

WEBSTER: Say, Reverend, you got a few minutes to spare?

TEMPLE: Why, hello Bruce. You bet I have.

WEBSTER: Well, if you got a couple minutes, there's something I want to ask you about. Something I want your advice on.

TEMPLE: All right. If you want to, we can talk in my car, and I'll drop you off at your place.

WEBSTER: That's fine.

While the car ride was in progress, the discussion was of a casual nature. Mr. Webster seemed to show some hesitation at raising his concern. They parked in front of the house where Webster lived with some people of high status in the community.

WEBSTER: Before I tell you what I got on my mind, Reverend, promise me you won't tell Joe and Nina. Don't tell nothing to them will you?

TEMPLE: Whatever you tell me, Bruce, I'll keep to myself. I promise.

WEBSTER: There's nothing the matter with colored folks is there, Reverend?

TEMPLE: Not to my way of thinking. They're human beings.

By this time Temple should have seen that Webster was genuinely concerned about something. And in his last comment Temple has done all right on the matter of convictions. Negroes are not queer or wrong just because they are Negroes, Webster has said. Temple finds nothing to correct so far as Webster has gone.

WEBSTER: That's what I figure. But some folks seem to think they got no feelings, that they don't laugh like ordinary people. They can't help it because their skin's black, can they?

TEMPLE: No more than you and I can help the color of ours (*still on the beam*).

WEBSTER: Joe and Nina and other people in town tell me I shouldn't have anything to do with them colored folks. Now if I'm doing something I hadn't ought to, I want to know about it. I want you to tell me.

Webster's concern begins to come into the open. He is being criticized for associating with the Negroes. At this point there might have been some temptation for the pastor, who was opposed to segregation, to say, "Don't pay any attention to them, Bruce. Just follow your convictions. If you want to associate with Negroes, do so." But no one with the slightest training in counseling would try to answer any question before its real nature has been disclosed. To do so would close off any further discussion of the conflict, and there is a conflict or Webster would not need help on it. Temple, knowing a little about counseling, had heard that you should not give answers to people's problems. As we shall see, he did not understand the dynamic meaning of this principle very well.

TEMPLE: Well, Bruce, I don't know whether I can or not. To tell you the truth, I don't know very much about the conditions down in that section.

This is evasive neutrality.

WEBSTER: I don't do nothing down there, just talk to the men. There's nothing the matter with them people.

TEMPLE: I suppose not.

WEBSTER: We just talk. Maybe they'll offer to buy me a drink, but I always tell them, "No, I don't want nothing. If you want to drink, go ahead. But I don't want nothing."

TEMPLE: They drink, but you don't.

The pastor apparently has his teeth clenched and is telling himself, "No matter what, don't say what you think." He concentrates so hard on keeping his views out that he is looking neither at Webster nor at Webster's views.

WEBSTER: That's right. Once in a while I may buy them a drink. But I never take any myself. Is it wrong for me to buy them drinks?

Webster is trying to clear out what he regards as the false attributions of his problems, believing the pastor's convictions would be against his associating with the Negroes if it were true that he drank, gambled, or had sex relations with them.

TEMPLE: Well, I don't know, Bruce. Do they expect you to buy drinks?

WEBSTER: No, I just want to be friendly. I watch them play cards and talk things over with them. They offer to buy me lots of drinks, but I always tell them, "No, I don't want nothing." If I'm doing any harm, I want you to tell me, Reverend.

TEMPLE: I doubt that I'm in position to do just that. Perhaps you wouldn't want me to, even if I could. You know what goes on down there better than I do, and you do have the right to choose your own friends. All I can say at present is: Use your best judgment.

WEBSTER: I always try. Well, I've got to be going in now. Nina'll think I got lost. Thanks a lot, Reverend, and don't tell nobody, will you?

TEMPLE: You're welcome, Bruce. Don't worry. I'll keep this to myself. Don't hesitate to let me know if you want to talk some more.

As counseling this is a flop. Temple concentrates so hard on his not giving Webster an answer that he does not succeed in bringing out of Webster what may help in clarifying his conflict. In his evaluation Temple wrote, "My purpose was not to tell Bruce what to do." This negative goal so dominated his outlook that he got nowhere positively in what needed to be done.

The remainder of Temple's evaluation is instructive. "I hoped through conversation to enable Webster to achieve some understanding of his own feeling in relation to the circumstances prevailing in the Negro district. After all, Bruce was not involved in any heinous sin. On the contrary, he was, I believe, simply seeking to satisfy a normal need for social contacts. The Negro laborers were his friends, not the best friends he might have had, but nonetheless his friends. He went to see them because there he had a certain status, was respected, his presence appreciated. Racial prejudice was of no consequence to him. He had found a group of individuals who were willing to accept him as he was and with whom the lines of communication were open.

"It has since occurred to me that my responses were not as effective as they might have been in encouraging him to express himself freely. However, I was determined not to make a decision for him, either to justify his conduct, which would have pleased him, or to tell him that he should have refrained from visiting the district. In either case, had he accepted my judgment, I would have done an injustice to his capacity, limited though it may have been, for independent action."

Temple saw that there was an underlying reason for Webster's association with the Negroes, feeling at home with them as he did not with his own class, the upper crust. He also saw correctly that telling Webster he should or should not continue these associations would solve nothing. He even understood, on writing up the contact and reflecting upon it, that he had done nothing to help Webster clarify it. He does not indicate how he might have done better.

Temple said that racial prejudice meant nothing to Webster. By this he seems to mean that a prejudice against Negroes as Negroes was not a part of Webster, and that Webster's problem has little or nothing to do with race. Or, this is a personal problem, not a problem of convictions.

This seems to misunderstand both this situation and convictions about race. Little children, left alone, will play happily with other little children regardless of their race. It is social pressures and convictions taught them by their elders which make them prejudiced. Webster is now undergoing such indoctrination. On the other hand, he is under pressure from his inner, psychic life, which gets satisfaction out of association with people where he can feel at home. All prejudice develops out of some kind of combination of inner need and social pressure.

It is true that Webster's problem is clearly personal. If the pastor had helped him to get the pressure business out for examination, he might well have helped him to feel more secure in looking at what he wanted to do. In that case the chances are that Webster would have continued some associations with the Negroes but on a more enlightened and less compulsive basis. But if this had occurred, the prejudice situation would have been helped as well. Prejudice is prejudgment. It would be a prejudice to feel one could have no associations with Negroes. But it would also be a prejudice to feel that one's associations should be with people with whom one feels at home—regardless of any other considerations. If prejudice is to be broken down, a wall must be broken down. One does not break it down by climbing over to the other side.

Suppose we assume that the pastor had no interest at all in helping Webster, that his sole interest was in diminishing racial prejudice. In that case what would he have done? If Webster had continued his associations with the Negroes in defiance of the upper crust, little would have been gained, for the latter would simply interpret this as Webster's climb over the wall. If Webster had broken up the associations, the upper crust would have been pleased; but Webster would merely have backed away from the wall. But if Webster had help in clarifying his inner conflict, and could discriminate the personal needs and social pressures so that he could have uncompulsive association with the Negroes, then Webster's action would start the wall coming down. Therefore the action which would do most against racial prejudice would also, at the same time, best help Webster.

This sheds light on the more general problem with which we began, the place of the pastor's convictions in counseling. As we have seen from the Webster contact, it is impossible and undesirable for the minister to shed his convictions about the evils of race prejudice and segregation. It is equally impossible, as Temple demonstrated, to profess a neutrality on these which one does not feel. It would not have helped in the least if the pastor had pounded with his fist and urged Webster to defy the upper crust. This might have cleared the pastor's own conscience, but it would not have helped either Webster's dilemma or the general racial situation.

Provided the pastor's convictions made sense, and provided Webster was really seeking help, then the better counseling that could be given, the more likely it is that Webster would approximate Temple's convictions.

Even in counseling we need have no apology for our convictions, social or ethical or theological. Provided they are not of the legalistic variety, they have something to say about the superiority of moving in this general direction rather than that if people are capable of it. We are then interested in the direction of movement, not just in the reaching of some fixed and arbitrary point. If Webster cannot move so far or fast as someone else, this is of no moment, provided Webster is moving in the generally right direction. If we believe this is, for example, against racial segregation rather than for it, let us not apologize even in counseling. But we may be concerned that we do what is necessary to help the Websters move in this way, and not just verbally clear our own consciences without producing change of attitude in those with whom we deal.

FRIENDSHIP IN COUNSELING

Chapter Twelve

$\mathcal{C}$AN THE PASTOR COUNSEL WITH PARISHIONERS who are also his friends? If so, what are the special opportunities and the particular dangers? If not, why not? These questions have arisen in many forms in almost every group of ministers or theological students where I have discussed counseling.

The basic answer to them is not difficult, and goes something like this. First, distinguish between friendship and friendliness. Friendliness plainly refers to the approach of warmth, genuine interest, and real concern for people which is as important in counseling as in any other aspect of the pastoral relationship. Friendship, personal and intimate, is different. It is not merely a relationship to which the pastor gives something, but also one from which he gets something. His personal friends are, so to speak, those with whom he is willing to take off his shoes. Friendship is a personal and mutual relationship.

Seen in this way, counseling cannot be friendship. For the essence of counseling is that two people agree, at least for stated periods, to concentrate their attention on the

147

problems, interests, concerns, and values of one. If a personal friend says he does not like oysters, I may reply that I think he is missing something. If I am his pastoral counselor, we will both agree to explore whatever emotional or spiritual significance is contained in his antipathy to the bivalve. This tells us, then, that we cannot have personal friendship and counseling in operation at the same time.

There is still the question whether the pastor can, with a personal friend, redefine the relationship temporarily into a counseling one when the friend needs it. I would see no general reason why this could not be done in many situations. The point would be whether both persons understand and accept the limitation which the counseling places temporarily on the relationship. On the other hand, the pastor does well to recognize that it may be more difficult to do effective counseling with personal friends, no matter how explicitly the relationship is redefined.

So much for the general statement. What has been said above assumes that the pastor knows who are his personal friends and who are not. But in practice it seems to me the greatest confusion between friendship and counseling comes when the pastor does not recognize that at least part of his relationship with some people is motivated by personal friendship, that is, he gets something out of it for his own emotional needs.

An interesting interview throwing light on this problem has come to me from a young assistant pastor. He is a man of very good intellectual equipment, real perception in counseling and human relations generally, and a genuine warmth as well as charm of personality. Here is what he wrote about his previous contacts with Betty:

"Betty is an unusually attractive girl, very talented artistically, very well dressed, and extremely well mannered. She is about nineteen. Her father is well-to-do and a member of the church. Betty and I have always had a sort of special friendship and understanding. I knew she was to leave for college this fall; but about two weeks after school opened she turned up in church again with her family. When I said, 'Back for a vacation already?' she answered, 'No, back for good,' while her mother looked on rather embarrassed. After church I whispered to her that there must be a story here, and she whispered back that there certainly was and that she'd tell me about it sometime. A few days later I happened to be taking her home after an evening meeting and the following took place."

PASTOR: You promised to give me the story.

BETTY: Oh, I'm so ashamed I don't want to talk about it much. I've made such a fool of myself. But I just couldn't stay at that place.

PASTOR: Was it very large?

BETTY: No, not so large. And they were all so smart because they had gone to private schools, and when the dean said we were expected to study six hours daily outside of classes, I just knew I couldn't take it. I bluffed my way all the way through high school, and I knew that it would catch up with me.

PASTOR: You felt that you couldn't keep up with the academic standards of the other girls?

BETTY: Well, not that exactly. Oh, I don't know what it was. My family thought at first it was Joe, but that definitely had nothing to do with my coming home. They thought for a while that I was going to run away with him and get married, but Joe didn't enter into it at all.

PASTOR: Does Joe know that he didn't enter into it, or does he think he is the major reason?

From the point of view of counseling we can see that the pastor gets off the track at this point and distracts Betty. Nevertheless, she goes on with her problem.

BETTY: Oh, he knows. He's about the only one who seems to understand at all. My family sure didn't, and they don't completely understand it yet, although things are better than they were at first. But my father took it awfully hard. He's always wanted all his children to get to college, and ever since I was in grade school he has talked about how important it is to get good grades. Every time I brought home a B or a C, he'd say: "You'll never get into college like that." And I was just afraid.

PASTOR: Just the idea of being in college after that sort of build-up was enough to make you uneasy. (*Here the lead is followed very well.*)

BETTY: Well, that's part of it anyhow. I can't explain it all somehow, and I feel that no one will ever understand it all. The worst part was the way my family took it.

At this point Betty went into detail about the response of her family and its individual members. At first they were shocked, then felt ashamed and told Betty so; then everyone dissolved in tears. Especially was her father unforgiving, he and Betty not speaking for several days. Father finally worked himself up to a pitch and issued an ultimatum to Betty that she would have to leave if things did not change. He had overreached himself, however, for the next day he came penitently to Betty and asked her to go on a long ride with him.

BETTY: I was never so close to my father as I was on that ride. And I think both Father and Mother are being reconciled to the fact that I am not going to be in college this year.
PASTOR: What are your plans for this year?

This is diverting, leading off into the externals of the situation instead of concentrating on Betty's conflict and inner feelings.

BETTY: I am working as a receptionist, and I love it. I'm in contact with so many people, and there's so much to be done and so much to learn, and my boss is so nice. And the best part about it is that I'm earning my own money, and I like that. I've always had everything given to me, and so much that I didn't want it. So if I go to college now, I'm going to pay my tuition, or at least part of it.
PASTOR: This feeling of independence is very important to you?

Here the pastor almost follows the lead, but overdoes it. It would have been better to say: "You mean you're getting something from this experience now you've never had before?"

BETTY: Yes, it certainly is. One thing I really hate is the fact that I went back on my word. I said I'd go back and try it for

151

a few more days, but I couldn't stand the stares of the other people in school, and I left again after only two days and I'm sorry I went back on my word. And the other thing I hate is the way all my family are taking this. The other day I got on the bus and sat down next to my mother's cousin. She's a frustrated old maid, and I talked to her all the way downtown, and she didn't speak to me once. Just before she got off, she turned to me and said: "I suppose you know you are slowly killing your mother." That almost killed me. But I'm about over it now, and things are much better.

PASTOR: You feel that your parents are becoming reconciled to the situation?

BETTY: Yes, the whole thing is clearing up, and life is much simpler now. Well, I guess I'd better go in now. (*They had stopped to talk in front of Betty's home.*) Tell me, do you think I'll go to college?

PASTOR: Ever since I first heard you speak at church, I've said to myself: "Betty's got what it takes." I think you'll do what is the best thing in the long run.

BETTY: Thanks for everything. Thanks a million. Good night.

PASTOR: Good night.

When the pastor came to evaluate the contact, he showed some real insight. "I knew that Betty had been under some strain, and felt that perhaps I could help. She knew that I was sincerely interested; so my blunt first question was not resented. There must have been a better way of getting to the problem, but I couldn't think what it would be."

We could agree with the pastor here. He knew she had some confidence in him, and a direct approach meant cards on the table.

152

The pastor wrote further: "My next question was rather irrelevant, but I was trying to let her see that I was interested in the circumstances of her problem, and this was a rather unconscious method I chose."

But this question, about Joe, led to externals. Still, the relationship was not injured.

"My question about Joe's knowledge about the motives of her actions was to try to throw the situation into such a light that she would see that she had some responsibility to make the situation clear to him, but I don't think that the query advanced this conversation to any degree."

The pastor, perhaps because of youth, suspected a romantic rat and got off the track trying to smell it out. But the problem was only slightly, if at all, in that realm.

"In analyzing the entire contact I don't feel that I got to the bottom of her problem; for each time I would make a statement trying to understand what she had said, she would reply: 'Well, not exactly,' or, 'That's along the line of what I mean.'"

This troubled him very much, and unnecessarily. Such statements do not necessarily mean the pastor did not get the point, but often do mean that, being understood so far, the parishioner can go on to tell more explicitly what she really means. As a matter of fact, she replied in this way when he did follow leads, and in another way when he did not. He got the meaning of the two reversed. He concluded his evaluation:

"But I do think there is some value in letting her see that, although she knows I am in favor of college for her,

153

I do not condemn her for what she has done, nor do I think it is an irremediable step she has taken. On the other hand, my last comment was not good. But I still don't know what I could have said under the circumstances."

It is obviously important that Betty feel the pastor is not against her because of her not being in college. He believes, correctly, that it may be just as well to go out of his way in making this clear. The resort to doing this by mere verbal reassurance is not effective, however, and he senses this is so even if he does not know why. He has a curious feeling that, even though he has shown understanding and a good approach through most of the contact, with major exceptions we have noted, the whole thing has not come off. But here too he does not know why.

The answer to the larger question seems to lie in the fact that this is partially a friendship situation not recognized by the pastor as such. If we read again the pastor's statement in which he first introduces us to Betty, we are struck by some of the adjectives. Betty is "unusually attractive." She is "very talented artistically." She is "very well dressed." She comes from an upper-class or upper middle-class family. She and the young pastor have had "a sort of special friendship and understanding." Under other circumstances this might suggest a romantic interest. But this was not the case here.

What the pastor actually reveals to us in these opening comments is something like this: "Betty is a girl in my class"—whether class be interpreted in the sociologist's sense or in a more general way. Or it is as if he said to himself: "Betty is the kind of girl with whom I can share assumptions. She's my kind of person." This does not need to have any romantic angle attached.

We note the "sort of special friendship and understanding" and the whispering. What strikes us is that the young pastor is getting something emotionally out of this relationship, that it's a good deal more fun for him to talk with Betty than he would find it to talk with, for example, Alice who works at Woolworth's, wears gaudy clothes, is without artistic pretensions, and overdoes the lipstick.

But when Betty begins to talk about her situation, the pastor does, with exceptions noted, manage to follow her leads and make a beginning at helping her clarify her feelings. The acute period of her trouble came immediately after her return from college. That is now past. High emotion has been replaced by something which makes a calmer consideration possible. The pastor senses this, does not do a bad job in moving toward clarification. Nevertheless he correctly concludes that something stood in his way.

Betty, he would have admitted readily enough, was more interesting to him than most of the other young people. But he would have said: "Why shouldn't she be? She has something most of them don't have." He might have added: "I can make a reference or an allusion, and Betty gets it. With most of these kids I have to draw it in pictures." That is, the relationship gives him something because it represents an economy of effort, being able to take some things for granted, the assumption that things will be understood and agreed with, the existence of a large basis of agreement and mutual understanding from which to start. Betty is his kind of person.

But "his kind of person" does, among other things, go to college. Therefore, the more reliance this relationship places on the unspoken assumptions of friendship, the more Betty will conclude that she has broken the standards of the "class" which they both represent. Not understanding this, the pastor, in spite of following the counseling rule book for the most part, senses that something important is missing.

Had I been this pastor, I would have sought first to clarify these feelings in my own mind. Then, at some appropriate point in our chat, I would probably have said to Betty something like this: "As I get it, Betty, here is the way you feel now—this way and that. Now, you and I have been friends. There are a lot of things we can take for granted together. You know that, other things being equal, I would be for college. But we're not talking merely as friends now, and we're not talking about college in general. We're talking about Betty, and trying to help you assimilate this rough experience you've had so that, whatever you do in the future, you'll know better what's going on. This is what we mean by clarifying our feelings."

It might not be in one gulp, but this would be the kind of redefinition of the situation I would attempt to make as we went along, whether in this contact or another. As it is, this contact dribbles off. And now that Betty is precisely at the point where real clarification could be both possible and helpful, the pastor does not know what to do.

The real point is, then, that an element of friendship in a counseling situation, if not recognized for what it is, may throw things off the track. The moral is not the renunciation of personal friendship, even in the pastor's own parish, but clearer insight into what is friendship as against friendliness, that is, what relationships do something to meet the pastor's own emotional needs.

We sometimes speak of friendship as a relationship in which we can give up something gladly, can sacrifice, can lose ourselves in love and loyalty. That is all true and important. But it is the fruit, not the root, of friendship. The fact is that, even in sacrificing for a personal friend, we get something out of it. We have identified with him; and in doing something for him, even at an apparent loss to ourselves, we are gainers in an emotional sense.

The root of friendship is mutuality. It is a two-way relationship in which the emotional needs of two people get some satisfaction. It is fostered by shared likes and dislikes, tastes and distastes, assumptions for and against. The degree of agreement on things necessary for friendship may vary enormously with circumstances. Joe Green, in Lancaster, Pennsylvania, might meet Will Brown of the same city and find nothing in common of sufficient importance to prompt even a lunch together. But let him meet Will in Shanghai or Moscow, and the discovery that both are from Lancaster may set the wheels of friendship trundling apace. Many humorists have been alert to this tendency.

Our values, positive and negative, are nowhere seen more clearly than in our friendships—especially, as in the pastor and Betty, our friendships of whose friendship character we are only dimly aware. To bring home the dynamics of this, I have sometimes used the term "mutual prejudice." This is startling, but it has point. A prejudice is a judgment made prior to examination of the evidence. A mutual prejudice is such a judgment by two people of each other. If I find, in conversation with my dinner partner, that she believes theology should not be as pessimistic as Barthianism, that we need more and not less democracy, that Whittaker Chambers is certainly a peculiar fellow, and that she considers the clergy underpaid—I am quite likely to assume, prior to examination of her views on summer cottages or international relations, that they will be "right," that is, like mine.

There is nothing wrong with this process so long as I know what is going on. In deeper form than the caricature above, it is shared interests and disinterests which make friendship possible. But we need to look not only at what it leads to positively, but also at the limitations it brings if its processes remain unknown and unexamined.

The sociologists have underscored what we suspected anyhow, that the most difficult leap of the imagination for the ordinary citizen is genuinely to understand the value assumptions of people in another class group. Think, for instance, of the attempt of a *nouveau riche* who tries to find his way into the inner assumptions of the traditional upper class and succeeds only in evidencing "conspicuous consumption." Or think of the lower middle-class person, preoccupied with respectability, who finds it utterly impossible to understand the daily trek of the workingman to a near-by saloon.

These groups do not begin with shared assumptions, and they succeed in understanding those of the other group only if a purposive and intelligent effort is made to do so. Of course friendship may transcend class lines, but this shows only that there are common values beneath the differences, not that the differences do not exist.

One is tempted to some general remarks on this subject beyond the counseling reference. In this country we have prided ourselves on the absence of any permanent class barriers, in contrast to a caste system. This is immensely important. But we have classes just the same, which are no less influential in setting patterns of value and conduct for our reluctance to discuss their significance. It is as if we feared that admitting their existence would itself perpetuate their power. The fact is that they operate more powerfully, and dangerously, the less we face them as facts.

As Erich Fromm has ably pointed out, the final test of love in the broadly human sense is whether we can love the "stranger," who is, generically, the person who does not necessarily share many of our most basic assumptions and values. This has nothing to do with setting aside our own values and adopting his. It is whether what we might call our friendship-capacity becomes capable of transcending kinship or "mutual prejudice" in such matters as dislike of oysters, giving equal value to a daily bath, kinds of food liked—and moving on to a recognition of mutual interests and assumptions in a more basic sense. Seen in this way, friendship-capacity is something which should not be reactionary, standing unexamined on what it has been taught to take for granted. Instead, it is something which needs cultivation—more cultivation in an interdependent world than ever before.

Friendship, to return to our original question, has no place in counseling in the sense that it is a mutual meeting of human and emotional needs. During these sessions at least, counseling is a relationship in which two people concentrate on meeting the needs of one. It is a special, auxiliary relationship—not life, but preparation for life.

But the pastor is a human being too, with flesh and emotions and needs like unto those he would help. He also needs friends. He should have them, and know who they are. He should not deceive himself into confusing the friendliness necessary in all his contacts with personal friendship. Nor should he think that, as a pastor, he has no need for close friendship. If he can make these distinctions, he will not be misled, as was Betty's pastor, into confusing counseling and friendship to the benefit of no one.

EMPATHY IN COUNSELING

*W*HAT DOES "EMPATHY" MEAN, AND WHAT place does it have in counseling? Rollo May is perhaps chiefly responsible for directing the attention of pastors to this idea, for in his well-known book *The Art of Counseling* (1939) he called empathy the "key to the counseling process." I suspect that he might now consider this an extravagant assertion. Nevertheless, the idea is important and merits reconsideration.

"Empathy" comes from the two Greek words for "in" and "feeling" or "suffering." It comes into English by way of the German word *Einfühlung*. The main root is the same as in the word "sympathy," the prefix meaning "in" instead of "with." May, in 1939, distinguished these two words as follows: "But whereas sympathy denotes 'feeling with' and may lead into sentimentality, empathy means a much deeper state of identification of personalities in which one person so feels himself into the other as temporarily to lose his own identity."

In contrast to May's idea, Harry Stack Sullivan in 1940 characterized empathy as the way a young child feels his way into identification with other people in the period before rational and analytical processes become important. It reaches its intuitional peak, he felt, at about the age of six, and thereafter declines. Since he felt that the later processes (beginning in preadolescence) which make a child increasingly capable of identifying the interests of selected others with his own were of a different order, he did not use the word "empathy" in that connection. And he did not use it in connection with psychoanalytic therapy.

The psychotherapeutic workers have been suspicious of empathy as of sympathy, and with some reason. For experience has shown that a counselor who becomes emotionally entangled with his patient or client loses the perspective which is necessary if he is going to be helpful. If Mr. Smith's account to me of his wife's atrocities so arouses my feeling for him that I forget my own task with him—helping him to clarify the situation so he can operate on whatever areas of it are open to him—then I am not really helpful to him at all. Even though empathy may not have so many sentimental overtones as sympathy, it is still a dangerous notion.

There is, however, something which is essential in counseling and for which we may use the word "empathy" until a better is devised. Let us first put this quality into negative terms. A counselor cannot succeed if he assumes he is merely manipulating a mechanical process, if he has the illusion that he can keep his own personality entirely out of the relationship, if he proceeds on a narrowly rationalistic basis, or if he tries to deny to himself that he has intuitive responses—positive or negative—toward the people he tries to help.

To put it positively but unsystematically, the counselor needs some genuine warmth of personality, the ability to convince his parishioner that he is genuinely interested in him and to have this true in fact, the capacity to lay aside temporarily his own problems and concentrate understandingly on the person and problems of the parishioner, and the ability to retain his sensitivity to the nuances of communication. For want of a better word, we might use "empathy" to describe the attitude the counselor attempts to achieve. I hold no great brief for the word. But if we use it at all, it ought to be for this.

Whether the word is to be used or not, the attitude itself is of great importance. I shall present parts of two pastoral interviews, in one of which the absence of empathy as defined above is the central failure, and in the other of which it is the reason for success.

The first interview is about Pastor Graves and Mrs. Mason. Mrs. Mason, a widow of forty-odd, owned the house in which she and her daughter lived, had a small income from a life insurance policy, but through a technicality had been barred from getting the pension which her late husband had built up. Recently she had been called on frequently by a man from another community, and the word of this courting had got around fast in the small town where Mr. Graves was pastor. Mrs. Mason sought out Mr. Graves one day; and after preliminaries had been taken care of, the following took place:

MRS. MASON: I have something that I have got to talk over with someone. I just don't know what to do.

GRAVES: Well, Mrs. Mason, I am at your service to talk over what is on your mind.

MRS. MASON: You know, Mr. Manners has been coming to see me almost every week end this spring?

GRAVES: Yes, I did see him with you at the Sunday service once or twice.

MRS. MASON: Well, I thought he was just a friend—but—well—he wants to marry me.

GRAVES: I see.

MRS. MASON: I don't know what to think about it. Mary is only fifteen and is still in school. She is all I have now. We have the house. We would have to sell it and move to Bigtown where Mr. Manners lives. I would have to take Mary out of school (*trailing off*).

GRAVES: It looks as though some changes would be necessary if you did marry?

MRS. MASON: And not only that. With the kind of insurance policy I have, it will stop if I get married.

GRAVES: You would feel that you were not independent to the extent that you are now?

MRS. MASON: What's that?

GRAVES: I mean that if you marry and sell the house and the pension stopped, you will not be as independent as you are now.

MRS. MASON: Yes, I think that is true.

GRAVES: You have thought through the possibilities on both sides, for and against the marriage.

MRS. MASON: Yes, I have. I just have to talk this over with someone. No one in the family will give me any help, and I just don't know what to do. You see, Mr. Manners is divorced, and he has two young children. He is working now and has promised to take care of all of us.

GRAVES: You indicate that Mr. Manners is not regularly employed?

MRS. MASON: Yes. What that had to do with the divorce, I don't know. I don't think he drinks. What the trouble was the first time, I don't know. He never said. He has a job now.

GRAVES: That is difficult.

MRS. MASON: This is the big risk that I can't figure out. I like him a lot; I believe in him. But this past of his—I don't know what to make of it.

GRAVES: That is a problem.

The discussion continued in similar vein. Then:

MRS. MASON: I guess that is my problem. I just hate to change my life here. Maybe it is the fear of the future that is really bothering me. I just hate to make a change. You see, I have already bought the license, and it will expire in three days.

GRAVES: That brings the problem right up to now, doesn't it?

MRS. MASON: That is why I wanted to talk to you. If it expires, I shall have to get another one.

GRAVES: Well, that will not be too difficult. I would think it is a minor problem compared to the step you are contemplating. Don't you think?

MRS. MASON: Yes, it is.

GRAVES: Part of life is adjusting to new situations and changes, it seems. You remember that section in the first part of *David Copperfield* where his aunt was preparing him for the death of his mother. It was a true statement of the changes that take place in one's life and the necessity for working them out through our total personality. You indicate that you have thought this through in part, that you love Mr. Manners, that you are thinking about marrying him. You have already bought the license. Now you are beginning to doubt and to hesitate. That does happen. It happens to all of us at certain times.

The interview continued. Mrs. Mason did not reach a final decision about the marriage during this contact.

In his evaluation Mr. Graves congratulated himself that he had not pushed her one way or the other toward a decision. He wished that she had made up her mind during the interview, but said he believed at least that he took "the pressure off the almost expired license."

At first glance it appears that Mr. Graves did not do badly. We see a number of attempts on his part to say in effect, "Then you mean so and so?" And yet a more careful reading shows that this is the shadow of understanding without the substance. Mr. Graves reflects on the issues, but in his terms, not those of Mrs. Mason. Witness the *David Copperfield* oration and "You indicate that Mr. Manners is not regularly employed?" These represent attempts to pick up things in order to clarify the central issue as it exists in his mind, not in that of Mrs. Mason. All the way through, in spite of the attempts to grasp her meaning, this is never really done. The climax is with the license. Mr. Graves misses the import of this entirely.

Reverting to our earlier discussion, we can say it is empathy which Mr. Graves entirely lacks in his dealing with Mrs. Mason. He acts mechanically, but cannot even achieve a mechanical reflection of feelings. He believes his personality is kept out of the picture if he does not push toward one decision or another. He is rationalistic, as for example in relation to the license, missing entirely the deeper overtones of meaning. He considers it a virtue to rule his intuitive responses out of account—as towards the irregular employment of Mr. Manners.

We get no sense of warmth or genuineness from the contact. Mr. Graves does not manifest to us or to Mrs. Mason genuine interest in her predicament and its uniqueness. He is insensitive at most points. And he does not succeed in concentrating well on her situation as she sees and feels it.

Had I been Mr. Graves, I would have been struck by the apparent fact that Mrs. Mason and Mr. Manners had communicated only superficial things to each other, as evidenced by their not having gone into Mr. Manners' past. So far as this material tells us, Mrs. Mason feels she must take this or leave it—which would mean entering a marriage with only superficial levels of communication as her right. Whatever the decision on marriage, this reluctance in Mrs. Mason tells us something about her. We could have empathy with her, but we would still ourselves not assume her perspective as the only one possible. At the point where Mr. Graves said, "That is difficult," we might have said, "I take it that you feel uneasy about this inability to talk over the past with Mr. Manners."

Just why Mr. Graves lacked the qualities which I have

collectively called empathy is not the object of our discussion. He was young, inexperienced, a bit stiff in personality, and with a very little knowledge of counseling was trying to get over his previous pattern which had been to tell people what to do. Seen as a stage in his learning, therefore, this is no doubt better than he had done before. But until he gets some ease, genuineness, and ability to empathize with what a parishioner is trying to communicate, he will be a mechanical rationalist in counseling.

In contrast we may look at the hospital call which Pastor Pierce made on Amos Carver. Mr. Pierce was calling on some of his parishioners who were in the hospital, and had also been asked by his friend, the hospital chaplain, to call on Mr. Carver. Amos Carver was a Negro in his mid-twenties. Unmarried, his father dead and his mother remarried, Mr. Carver has been going it alone for some years and without the benefit of either much intelligence or much education.

After Mr. Pierce had introduced himself as coming from the chaplain:

CARVER: I am just gittin' treatment for my ear. I'll be out soon; then I'm goin' back to see my aunt in Carolina, but I don' know what I'm gonna do. She's dependent on me. My mother's in Georgia. My father's dead. I'm here all by myself.

PIERCE: I guess you're feeling pretty much alone.

CARVER: Yeah, dass it. Don't have nobody to look to. But I git along. I always have, but I don' know—I jus' feel (*agitated, squirming in bed*).

PIERCE: Sort of like nobody cares.

CARVER: Yeah, dass what I mean. I got a friend of my mother's near here, and she give me lots of advice, and my cousin comes to see me once in a while.

PIERCE: But you don't feel very close to them?

CARVER: No, not exactly.

PIERCE: But you've always got along even though you feel pretty much alone.

CARVER: Yeah, since I was about so high. My mother's married agin, and she has a baby. I saw her just before Christmas. I git along 'cept when somebody mistreats me. Then I feel I ain't got nothing to live for—when somebody mistreat me.

PIERCE: Things seem kind of discouraging to you.

CARVER: Yeah, I feel down and low in my spirits. When I was living over on First Street and I was gittin' my twenty dollars a week from the gov'ment, I wasn't workin' and I didn' have no job. I felt by myself and sometimes you wanna do things you shouldn'. But I didn'.

PIERCE: You mean when you have something on your mind like a job you feel a lot better.

CARVER: Yeah, dass it. When I was workin', I come home at night, and I had something to think about for the next day. I didn' git restless, you know, and run aroun'.

This is enough to give us the flavor of the pastoral call. They swung into discussion of jobs, and there was some clarification of the kind of thing Mr. Carver might be able to do that was in line with his interests. A fear Mr. Carver had of the "social workers," especially in job-helping, was discussed helpfully. Some real groundwork was laid whereby Mr. Carver can take some steps on his own.

What strikes us about Pastor Pierce is his real empathy in the sense in which that has been defined here. Not only does he concentrate on Mr. Carver, but he is clearly doing so because he is genuine, warm, and interested in Mr. Carver. He does not confuse his own thoughts about the situation—for example, how limited are Mr. Carver's occupational opportunities—with Mr. Carver's feelings. Mr. Carver is in low spirits. Mr. Pierce can accept those feelings, understand them and show he understands, and emphathize in relation to them, but without sharing the feelings or the perspective which they represent. Accordingly, he is helpful, even with a man whose poor education and low intelligence make him more difficult for a person like the pastor to reach.

Although our task is not to give a character sketch of Mr. Pierce, it seems clear that part of the reason he can empathize in helpful fashion with Mr. Carver has something to do with having come to terms with his own inner life, and having followed through the implications of this in his pastoral work. He can give himself and his attention warmly and unreservedly, but without in any way losing his own perspective. He can move inside Mr. Carver's feelings and not be afraid of being found wanting because he is also, at the same time, outside those feelings.

If we should try too hard to feel our way into the feelings of a parishioner, we would be demonstrating not empathy but anxiety for our own place in the situation. If we pushed aside what is here called empathy, said it was of no importance and that only objectivity counted, we should be moving toward a purely mechanical view of counseling. If the kind of empathy which is helpful is to come, it results, as a by-product, from a combination of factors: our familiarity with ourselves, our clear understanding of the counseling process, sufficient feeling at home in that process that our self-esteem is not dependent on the degree of readiness for help of the parishioner, and enough intellectual understanding of the varieties of psychic experience that we do not jump to conclusions on the basis of how we would feel in a similar situation.

Empathy, then, is an ability, as the word implies, to feel our way inside the feelings of someone else—but only as we are quite content to have our own feelings firmly rooted outside that person. If we are to help him, we must be at home with his feelings in a way which he is not. But we can be so only if we are at home with our own.

There is certainly an intuitive element in empathy, in the sense that it does not proceed through a mere identifying in this situation of certain elements which one has also perceived in previous situations. There is always a certain alertness to novelty, to the fact that it may be as important to be alert to nuances of feeling as to identify broad types of feeling. No matter how advanced and exact our knowledge of personality and of counseling becomes, we shall never be able to sit back and rest in a subtle form of unalertness to the individuality of the parishioner we are trying to help. In this context empathy becomes not a substitute for whatever exact knowledge is possible, but an alertness to that which transcends any exact knowledge we have but which is nevertheless essential in the counseling process. In so far as what we learn from its exercise is in any sense knowledge, it may be called intuitive—provided it be not thereby exempted from examination by more rigorous processes of study.

In broader terms than counseling, empathy as here defined may offer some leads concerning the relationship between individuality and sociality, between selfhood and fellowship. For in a sound sense we can feel our way into the experience of another only to the extent that we have felt ourselves at home with our own experience. We can enter in only to the extent that we are content to remain out. We can have fellowship only as we accept our own selfhood.

PERSPECTIVE IN COUNSELING

*I*N THE MIDDLE OF THE SEVENTEENTH CENTURY the English clergyman George Herbert wrote these words in his book *A Priest to the Temple, or the Countrey Parson:* "The Countrey Parson hath not onely taken a particular servey of the faults of his own Parish, but a generall also of the diseases of the time, that so when his occasions carry him abroad or bring strangers to him he may be the better armed to encounter them."

If we are to be effective "countrey parsons" in our day, we too need to take "a generall also of the diseases of the time." We strive to be constantly aware of the individuality of each parishioner and his problems. But we need also to have a perspective on the "generall" with which our times afflict both him and us.

Each of us has his own way of talking about the general problem of our time as this is mirrored within the lives of individuals. Some think of this as rootlessness and not belonging, the uncomfortableness arising from having lost the old certainties and not yet having established the new. Others stress the feeling of insecurity, both pro-

ducing and resulting in various forms of regimentation—
at any rate the encroachment of stereotypes upon individuality. Some emphasize the root problem of the present
as anxiety, a panicky feeling of helplessness from which
escapes may be attempted in all directions. All these and
other ways of stating the problems have relevance.

Whatever appears to us the best way of stating the
general predicament of the individual peculiar to our
times, it is clear that this has something to do with the
impingement upon us of a wider world than in any past
time. War and the threat of war reach from every corner
of the globe and touch every person. The sense of economic insecurity increases as individuals have proportion-
ally less control over this aspect of their living, at the same
time seeing that economic plenty is possible for the first
time in history. Interracial relations are no longer a merely local problem, but affect the feelings of individuals
throughout the world. So in many realms of life.

If the positive potentialities—for peace, plenty, and
amity—were not so obvious, the "generall" of our times
might be despair and hopelessness, giving up the struggle.
But this is not true either for the world as a whole or for
the West. What gives poignancy to our general problem
is the contrast between the potentialities for good and
those for evil. At the very time when we see we can take
hold and bring a better world into being, we have doubts
about who "we" are, how we can take hold, and what we
want to bring about anyhow. The more we see that we
must find and exercise our freedom, the more tempted we

are to "escape from freedom," in Erich Fromm's phrase.

This chapter is of course about counseling and is not the presentation of a new analysis of the problem of our times, even of the individual. But it has been necessary to say this much in order that we may ask our particular question: What does our perspective on the general problem of our times mean in our counseling? How does our "generall" affect the work in our "own Parish"?

It is my belief that our counseling will be more realistic, more helpful, more compassionate, and more alert to individuality if its function and its methods are thought out in relation to our more general perspective on the "diseases of the time." That is, these two things are not to be held in logic-tight compartments, but considered in their relationships.

To suggest how this should and should not be done, I will draw upon two pastoral contacts which were had by a young minister who has a broad social perspective. He came from a southern background, is progressive in his views on social, economic, and racial questions. While taking graduate study, he needed a job just for the summer months. He came to the attention of Horace Wing, a supersuccessful businessman who is also chairman of the board of an exclusive summer colony.

For some years previously the colony had operated a chapel, but because of growing lack of interest on the part of the young adults the board had been thinking of not operating it this year. Yet they hesitated to abolish it, feeling this might be bad for the morale of the younger

175

set. The board felt that if they could get a young minister who could meet the young people on their own terms—play golf, and tennis, and swim—it would be worth while to continue the chapel program.

When the young minister, whom we may call David Lodge, came to talk with Mr. Wing, he was first interrogated about his own background and experience. From my observation I could say that even a man as smug as Mr. Wing turned out to be could see that Pastor Lodge was a person of intelligence, charm, and integrity. Then they swung into discussion of the chapel.

WING: Frankly, we've come to a road block as far as the chapel is concerned. Attendance got so bad last summer that we didn't even have regular services.

LODGE: You're about ready to close up shop, and yet you're hoping somehow to revive the religious interest of the young adults, is that it?

WING: Yes, but it's going to take some real reviving! Saturday nights out here are pretty wild, and the folks are in no mood to be preached at on Sunday morning.

LODGE: Then you want some one to work *with,* rather than preach *at,* them?

WING: We want a minister who knows how we live—who is willing to live with us—and who can talk in our language. Why, one minister we had out here hadn't even heard of the *Reader's Digest!*

At this point in writing it up Mr. Lodge introduced the following parenthetical note, "This minister had *something* in his favor."

LODGE: Then you want to be accepted for what you are, and also to be confronted with a religious message that speaks to your condition?

WING: Yes. Why, most of the younger crowd are not even sure religion *can* speak to their condition.

LODGE: They're not sure, but they still have a little hope?

WING: I guess maybe they do at that. All of them have some nominal Protestant affiliation. But some of us are pretty close to giving up on the possibility of getting anybody to come out here who can give us something meaningful *and* keep it interesting.

LODGE: There's still a spark left to be ignited, but it had better be done soon?

WING: I'll say—this summer in fact. We have to have a man we consider worth listening to, just like we would consider a good book worth reading.

LODGE: You want a man who holds your interest *and* makes you do some thinking—and perhaps acting too?

WING: (*nodding*) And we want short services, perhaps starting at ten o'clock so people could get in a round of golf before lunch.

LODGE: Short services, but worth getting up for?

WING: Right, and as I mentioned before, this may well be our last try. If the program falls through this summer, we'll close the chapel entirely.

LODGE: Your plans have real potentialities, Mr. Wing, and I'd *like* to tackle this job. You've got something of a Utopian view of a minister; but if, as you say, you want a man to meet these younger adults on their home grounds and try to suggest the relevance of the Christian faith to their lives, that means a challenge I want to *try* to meet.

The discussion continued about more detailed plans. Mr. Lodge did take the job and handled it very well. Without tempering his convictions at all, he did get the interest not only of the younger set but of many of Mr. Wing's contemporaries also.

In his evaluation Mr. Lodge wrote, "I went into this conversation inwardly critical of Mr. Wing and of the economic group and order which he represents. But I was determined above all else to get his side of the picture. I am convinced that he envisions Christianity and the church mainly as instruments for the preservation of values—his values, as reflected in the present economic order. However, he was concerned to carry on some kind of religious expression in the life of his community. This was a contact with a man who is in a very tangible way representative of the reactionary economic blight upon our social order. But his intentions are sincere and his convictions real. In any event, my only hope of bringing about a process of change is in first going to where he and his community are, then seeking to help them see their way clear to act more responsibly toward society in the light of their Christian faith."

This is not, of course, counseling but a precounseling pastoral contact of an administrative character. But if there is to be any chance of getting Mr. Wing and all the other smug Wings to a point where either counseling or Christianity can take hold, the issue is likely to be determined in contacts like this.

For my taste and convictions Mr. Lodge leaned backward too far in not clarifying his own position a little to Mr. Wing. He also seems to me a bit too sanguine about the positive element in Mr. Wing's convictions. I believe one could have been less passive with Mr. Wing and yet sustained a relationship with him.

Nevertheless, Mr. Lodge is on the side of the methodological angels. Consider what he might have done in this interview and in later life. On the one hand he might have gone down the line with Mr. Wing, setting his previous convictions aside. He might have confused understandstanding with agreement. His convictions might slowly have faded into the background, at least those which would create tension in ministering to upper-class parishioners. He might then have become the sort of wealthy-suburban-church pastor who feels at home there without tension. Actually, what such churches need is ministers who can make contact but who also lead—and preserve the tension.

On the other hand Mr. Lodge might have become indignant and told Mr. Wing then and there how atrocious he felt his social and religious views were. This would have cleared his own conscience, but done nothing for Mr. Wing or the summer colony. If Mr. Lodge had been impelled to do this, no doubt he would over a period of time have become a minister who felt comfortable only when dealing with the more or less underprivileged. In this, even as in its opposite, the criterion of whom he tried to serve would not be the need and opportunity—but his own sense of lack of tension.

In both instances he would have failed with Mr. Wing. What Mr. Lodge is trying to do is something like this: first, do his best to understand Mr. Wing and his point of view; second, keep his own perspective clear; third, then decide whether there are enough handles to grab so that he might or might not enter the situation. His own perspective becomes clarifying to the situation and therefore provides the best groundwork for later changing it, instead of crystallizing it more firmly by immediate acquiescence or opposition.

This same young minister chanced on a train to sit with a "stranger"—a Negro about thirty, a university graduate who had been forced to take up menial labor after returning from Army service and finding no opportunities in the field for which he was trained. We shall call him George Lewis.

In the casual conversation which Mr. Lewis and Mr. Lodge had at the beginning, Mr. Lewis showed a good deal of bitterness over his situation. When the fact emerged that Mr. Lodge was a minister, the following ensued:

LEWIS: You sure have a job ahead of you. For my money, give me a pagan over a church member almost every time. What good is all your preaching? It just seems to salve people's consciences so they can go on sinning.

LODGE: You've heard too much preaching and seen too little practice, eh?

LEWIS: Maybe. At least the preaching doesn't seem to lead to anything. But what I can't understand is how people can claim to believe in the Sermon on the Mount and go on cutting their brothers' throats.

LODGE: Yours is certainly the sixty-four dollar question for anyone who's really concerned over the problems we've been talking about. And you've had good reason to ask it.

LEWIS: I was a church member once myself, but I quit. My own race was just as hypocritical as the whites.

LODGE: You didn't feel you could belong to a group that wasn't measuring up to what it professed?

LEWIS: That's about it—not that I was any better than they were. But we kept on with the ways of the world, so why kid ourselves that we were really being religious!

LODGE: Then you don't think people should belong to the church unless they live up completely to its teachings?

LEWIS: Well, not completely, no. But it ought to make a difference in their lives. As I see it, it's hard to tell a Christian from a non-Christian. And even when you know, the non-Christian will often give you a better break.

LODGE: I sure agree with you that being a Christian ought to make a difference. But you feel it works the other way sometimes?

LEWIS: Sure. You take when I was looking for a job when I came home from the Army. Only place I was even considered was by a Jewish firm.

LODGE: Then you believe the discrimination others showed you was connected with their being members of the Christian church?

LEWIS: Could well be. The churches are segregated as badly as any other organizations—looks like the practice carries over into business and everywhere else in life.

LODGE: You sure put me on the spot. But I hope you won't give up your church entirely.

LEWIS: No, I can see it's got something if it'll only bring it out of the moth balls once in a while. But right now I have my doubts.

From this point on Mr. Lodge became too much interested in getting Mr. Lewis to come back to church, and the contact dribbled off.

Here too, apart from the conclusion of the contact, Mr. Lodge did a good job, and in the face of unusual difficulties. He had been reared in the South, so that his present position on race, which stemmed from his Christian conviction, had been hard-won. A "convert" is usually more eager to sustain his new position at all costs than is a person who has been reared with it.

His first temptation, therefore, was to agree with Mr. Lewis wholeheartedly, at least on his general thesis. He could easily have pointed out that Christianity for most people is a matter of respectability plus cosmic insurance, that real Christians cannot necessarily be identified by their church membership. Or if he had had a more neo-orthodox slant, he could have indicated that the Sermon on the Mount is an unrealizable ideal, that we must be impelled by it but can never reach it, that we are all caught in the same situation. This course of action would have made Mr. Lewis feel more at home with his Indignation Quotient, but it would not really have helped.

A second kind of temptation into which Mr. Lodge might have fallen would have been to tax Mr. Lewis for his own strategic short-sightedness while agreeing with his complaints. This would have been "realism." In effect he could have said, "I know all you say is true. And I feel as bad about it as you do. But we're all in the present situation. And *you* have a responsibility too. Every Negro who works until he gets the job he's trained for thereby helps his own race and, in the long run, all of us. It seems to me you've more or less given up trying to do anything yourself, and are just waiting for the rest of us to do something for you." This might well be a *goal*, for people like Mr. Lewis do have to live in the present situation and have to pull as much of an oar as they can get hold of if things are to be made better. But it is poor *strategy*, for it bumps quickly over Mr. Lewis' feelings.

Until the latter part of the contact what Mr. Lodge did was effective. He understood, did not read himself into it, and moved a few steps toward clarification in Mr. Lewis. At the same time Mr. Lodge did not lose his own perspective. Mr. Lewis' problem is both individual and supraindividual. There are things he can do about it and things which can be done only by action far transcending his own. Because he does not lose sight of this fact, Mr. Lodge moves in the direction of helping Mr. Lewis to do whatever can be done by himself about his situation. But he is equally clear that this is not all that needs to be done.

In principle these contacts seem to me to suggest how our perspective on the general problem of individuals in our time can enter appropriately into our counseling. We do not become indignant against the person, although we may well define the difference between his view and ours. We attempt not to have the relationship broken. But neither will we try to cement the relationship by crawling into someone's ideological mud puddle with him. We can understand his view, maintain our own perspective, and utilize our pespective to help both him and the wider situation.

For the "generall" of our times has affected both Mr. Wing and Mr. Lewis. Our sympathies are against the former and for the latter. Yet we know that their views have been evolved under the pressure of the times, that each in his own way has experienced the fact or the fear of rootlessness, of insecurity, of anxiety, of the impinging of a wider world upon his condition. This is a fact, not an excuse for the *status quo* in either. But this means that there are reasons for their views in their experience; and if Mr. Wing is to change his views, and Mr. Lewis to become capable of taking such action as is open to him, the people themselves must be understood. So the perspective on the "generall" helps both individually and generally.

The theologian might well go on from this point and say that there is a "generall" of a still deeper kind originating in man's cosmic situation and not just out of his times. This is true, even though we might háve as many ways of describing this as the "diseases of the time." The perspective would then be still broader. But in terms of counseling the place of this perspective would be the same. Fundamentally we do not help either by becoming indignant against the one who does not believe as we, or by merely snuggling up to him who does. Instead we can utilize this perspective to help both him and the wider situation.

We need to discover and to hold firmly our own social and theological perspectives. But the implication of my analysis is that we do this soundly as Christian pastors only if we have gone far enough to do it "operationally." It is not enough to know what we believe, though that is necessary. If our beliefs are to mean anything, then they need to be considered strategically in relationship to the various forms of our ministry, of which counseling is one. To have social and theological perspective over there and counseling method somewhere else is not enough. I believe that in the exercise of our Christian ministry, if properly understood, each helps the other.

INDEX

(The following ideas and concepts are so pervasive throughout this book that it was found impossible to index them without referring to every third or fourth page: compulsion as against freedom, the dynamics of counseling, following leads in counseling, alertness to expressed feelings, understanding, and the communication of understanding. Accordingly, their absence from the index is an indication of their significance and not the reverse.)